JONATHAN CHAMBERLAIN has lived most of his life in Hong Kong and Ireland but now lives in Brighton, England. In addition to his writing, he has founded two charities for families with mentally handicapped children, one of which is influencing the development of family-based services in China. He is also an activist for alternative approaches for cancer and to this end he has a website at *www.fightingcancer.com* and a blog at *cancerfighter. wordpress.com*.

WORDJAZZ FOR STEVIE

How a profoundly handicapped girl gave her father the gifts of pain and love

Jonathan Chamberlain

BLACKSMITH BOOKS

Wordjazz for Stevie

ISBN 978-988-17742-7-9

Published by Blacksmith Books
5th Floor, 24 Hollywood Road, Central, Hong Kong
Tel: (+852) 2877 7899
www.blacksmithbooks.com

Also by Jonathan Chamberlain:

Non-fiction
Chinese Gods: An Introduction to Chinese Folk Religion
Cancer: The Complete Recovery Guide
Cancer Recovery Guide: 15 Alternative and Complementary Strategies
for Restoring Health
King Hui: The Man Who Owned all the Opium in Hong Kong

Fiction
Whitebait & Tofu

ACKNOWLEDGEMENTS

Bern and I could not have survived the difficult early years of Stevie's life, and I could not have survived the time of Bern's illness and after, without the support and kindnesses – large and small – of many people, far too many to name. You know who you are. I owe a profound debt of gratitude to you all.

S tevie, my love, how can I explain it?

It was the love and the pain. Both together. In a single moment there was an absolute separation of past and present. A total dislocation. It was as if... But this is not a story to tell a child. Ah! But Stevie, you are no longer a child, you are an immortal.

How can I explain it?

Imagine a man walking down a road. He is not going anywhere important. Just walking, not thinking. Then suddenly, something happens. For a second he has a superconsciousness of some absolute, irrevocable event taking place... of something that is inescapable, that is going to happen before it all clarifies in his mind. There is no time for action. Only time to acknowledge. Somewhere between one beat of his heart and the next he is aware of a dialogue; a dialogue, he senses, between the person he was a moment ago and the person he is about to become.

And then there is the explosion. A cosmic roar. Here, in the middle of the sound, he knows he is being ripped apart. Sound and pain are one. He knows that now, finally, he has been given his own fate.

Then, as he attempts to escape the pain, slowly, grudgingly, uncomprehendingly, he becomes aware that he is holding something. He turns his head to see if this is true, that he is indeed grasping something. His mind is operating in a dull fashion. It appears he is able to take hold of only one thought at a time – and each thought gives way to the next most reluctantly. He turns his head and fixes his gaze on his hand. It is true that it appears to be clasping something. What he is clasping he cannot imagine. Whatever it is, it is hidden within the fist that is gripping it tightly with an almost spastic intensity. Slowly he understands that he needs to send a command to his fist to relax and then for the fingers to ease open like a flower blossoming. First he sees the problem. Then he sees what he must do. Then, he realises he must do it. And then he does it. He issues an instruction and somewhere along the chain of command a switch is thrown and his hand is told to bring forth the fruit. Only then does the hand unfurl.

He opens his hand and there in the palm of his hand, resting in the leathery creases, is a large glittering stone as large as a small bird's egg and filled with light.

At first he doesn't give the object a name. It is simply something that draws him in. For a long time, the very longest time, he is not aware of anything else apart from this clear, etched, limpid stone rich in all the colours of the rainbow in their deepest and most profound form. He sinks into the shifting whorls of light and colour. He feels lightened, unburdened. His cares are stripped from him. And as he sloughs them off like a heavy winter coat, he feels his heart pumped full with love – a beating ecstasy, an overflowing richness of emotion. How can he explain this feeling? It fills him and overflows. He cannot contain it. He is aware that he is floating in a sea of pain and love, a pain that screams obscenities and a love that sings like birdsong. There he is, he says to himself, silently, wonderingly, because he has an image of it inside his mind as if it were outside his body, there he is floating on this terrible sea. How can this be? He hardly knows how to frame the question. He asks himself another question. How do I feel?

Indeed, how does he feel? Feel now? Now? What does now mean? This moment? This moment which has already escaped to become another moment, just another fleeting moment of the past? Focus on feeling, he tells himself. Love and Agony? Annihilation and completion. Emptiness and fulfilment. Both torn apart and put together. Mended and destroyed. Yes, yes, the pain. But also the love and laughter that poured out of his heart and didn't stop pouring out. A pure fountain of loving love. And the whole world was suddenly different. And the whole world and the rest of his life was made new again. And meaningful.

And Stevie, my dear Stevie, that man was me. And I was never able to separate the pain from the love. I did not know it then but the love was the key to the pain. The pain, of course, was the key to the love. And the name of the stone was Stevie. It was you. Did you already guess that? The life-transforming diamond of love and pain.

And, yes, Stevie, you too knew about pain and love and laughter.

What stories do little girls want to hear? Not stories of pain. You want to know how it all began. How did your mummy and I meet so that we could come together to have you as our baby?

Well, let's start at the beginning. I fell in love with your mother's perfect feet. It started with the toes – that perfect fan of strong even toes – and then moved back along the broad expanse of the foot to the neat ankle, then her calf. My love moved upwards slowly – thighs, buttocks, belly, breasts – until I loved all of her.

Some people fall in love the other way round. They love the face first and only later discover the feet. But that's the way it was with me. I fell in love feet first.

When I think back on those days I ache for the beauty of your mother's body and her movements against mine. Two young eager bodies desiring each other, giving fleshy pleasures to each other. There are whole afternoons that should be cryonically preserved.

But it wasn't just a matter of the hungers of flesh. Recently, looking through some photo albums I came across a photograph of your mother leaning back against a railing, wearing just T-shirt and shorts. The photograph was electric with her energy and the amused love light in her eyes. And I fell in love with her again.

And not just energy but spirit too. One day it was raining and we were down by the beach. It was deserted. We had a ball. And we started to throw the ball at each other, getting wet in the rain. And laughing. Fully dressed. Getting soaked. Throwing a ball. Being young and enjoying it.

Stevie, one of my favourite photographs of your mother was taken the night we were celebrating our engagement with a dinner to introduce both sides of the family to each other. Your mother wore a yellow-gold trouser suit with the high Chinese collar. There is the look of a fox in her eyes and such spirited beauty.

Recently, I came across an Indian story that describes the creation of womankind. God, said the creator of the story, took the beauty of flowers, the song of birds, the colours of the rainbow, the kiss of a light breeze, the laughter of the sea's waves, the gentleness of lambs, the cunning of the fox, the waywardness of the clouds and the fickleness of spring showers and wove them all together to make a wife for the first man.

This myth leaves out some important ingredients: a temper hot as fiery flames, a temper slow as burning embers, the obstinacy of stone.

That's what your mother was like.

And then there's the story about how it was that I came to ask your mother to marry me. This is a story that you must close your eyes to listen to. Yes, Stevie, even you.

Looking down from the rock. Sunlight skitters off the surface of the flat sea. The water is so inviting. So clean. The afternoon shivers with stillness. The moment becomes tense with expectation. It has taken many years to reach this moment of – no, not yet clarity, not yet. Not yet beginning. This is ending. Standing on top of the rock jutting out from the beach. Sunlight, silver and gold speckles on the slight ripples of the water that waft lazily in to the beach. A thought beckons. I am tempted.

That morning I had got on a boat that had headed out from the shore towards unseen islands. The heat of the day scorched down. I could smell the dirt sweat stink of my self-disgust. How to get rid of it, how to become clean again? I longed to plunge into the crystal, sparkling aquamarine water that the flimsy boat put-puttered through. Occasionally there was a spray and dance of flying fish. Just to stop the inevitability of time's onward rush. Just take one step and throw myself into the cooling, cleansing water. There would after all be no danger. The boat would stop. The captain – to dignify the burnt-black boat operator – would curse and mutter but what of it. But I didn't have the courage.

Then somehow, from the boat to a crowded conveyance to a point on the road and a long dirt path that led eventually to the beach and the small huts for rent and the rock that jutted out into the water a short way. And now here I was. Here I was at the ending that was about to end.

Why I had climbed up on to the rock I can't remember. I must have thrown myself into the sea the minute I could. I had taken a lean-to at the edge of the beach under the less than secure canopy of a coconut tree – a small raised floor and the ceiling just high enough to crouch in. Thinking back on it now I see myself tearing off the sweat-stained clothes, putting on a swimming costume and then running down to the water and plunging in. Of course. The ecstasy. The cleanness of the coolness, wetness, saltiness and the hot, glaring sunlight.

And then...?

And then, a little later, as the heat of the day lost its edge, I had gone to investigate the rocks. Up here I was a good fifteen feet up. The afternoon sun came glancing off the smooth mirror of the sea's surface. I remembered a game we had played at school. There had been an outdoor swimming pool, six foot deep at the deep end. At the side there was a roofed changing area. The kick was to dive in off the roof into the deep end of the pool. From eight or nine feet high you got to palm yourself off the bottom of the pool. There was no real danger to it. The only way you'd get hurt was not having your arms out in front of you – or maybe if you slipped your footing and hit the side of the pool. That was what gave the game an edge.

But now I was thirty years old and at the end of my tether.

I stood on the rock. Now that the idea had come to me that I might dive into the sea I looked down at the water to judge it. Down below there was a natural rock pool. From the way the lines of the rocks below bent, I guessed the water was about six feet deep. Deep enough if I just had the courage. But fifteen foot up, I was higher than the roof of the changing rooms. Could I do it?

I had arrived on the rock but my mind was still restless, on the move, running from the sense of distaste that had been with me for the last few days, weeks, months – this feeling that I wanted to wash off. Like an itch it had to be scratched. Couldn't ignore it. Still this momentum for doing things, for moving. The rock was too high. Even I could see that. Just a bit too high. It would need guts to do it. I hadn't even had the guts to throw myself off the boat into the deep smooth, clear, bluey-green sea. I was a coward. I was running away. Running away from what? Myself? Destiny? Fate? What did these words really mean? Just running aimlessly, going nowhere, not having the courage to reach out and choose, to just do something – something for myself that might define myself. Do something to prove to myself I was... what? Something to respect myself for afterwards, not the things that I had been doing that gnawed away at my self-respect. I looked down again. I could get hurt. If I was younger, perhaps? Coward, I told myself.

I was beginning to feel a bit silly now standing up there on the rock squinting down at the water, measuring, always measuring. Assessing the depth, assessing my courage, assessing the wellsprings inside that could opt for life and adventure, pride and glory, solid plain affirmation... or the continuing sense of failure and disgust. Was life going to go on as it had done, steadily eating away at the soul?

I stood on the rock and stared down at the clear pool of water below me. It was clear right to the bottom. Perhaps six foot deep. I wasn't used to looking at water this clear. I was twelve, fifteen feet up. Did I dare dive into six foot of water? I knew I could do it. It was a matter of curving the back as soon as you hit the water and padding yourself off the bottom with the palms of the hands. Was I scared? Yes, I felt the butterflies flutter in my stomach as I stared at the water. It was just a matter of taking a deep breath and doing it. Too much thought made you scared. Just do it. I wanted to do it. I wanted to prove myself. Confirm myself. Prove that this flight from fear was an aberration, that it hadn't undermined me. I was scared of being scared. Scared at how my being scared of life had stumped me. I was at a dead end. But don't think about that, I told myself, just the water. It beckoned me and I felt its pull. I readied myself on the rock's edge and stared down the fear that was rising. Before it could reach my brain and make me back down, make me fail again, I thrust myself away into the air, away from the land. It wasn't a high jack-knifing dive as much later I would recall it but a headlong plunge towards the water and the sand bottom...

If there is a beginning, this is it. I see myself caught in mid air. Behind me there is a long sandy beach. Nearby are rocks and coconut palms. The sky is a shocking dark blue. The sea stretches out, going from sandy green to ruffled dark. Beyond is the silence of death.

Caught in mid air I suddenly understood something very clearly.

I saw I was going to die. The water in the pool wasn't six foot deep. How silly of me. I could see that now as I plunged down. It was two, maybe three feet deep at most. I was going to die. I braced myself against death. I hit the water with my arms slightly bent to break the fall.

My hands ripped through the silvery sheen of the water's surface. The surface ruptured at the head's plummeting passage. I could see all this quite clearly. I was both inside and outside the experience. The forearms took the main brunt of the impact as I slammed against the sand. The body continued its descent. Another foot of water and I would have been alright. My forehead slammed against the sand bottom. My body jarred and fell around me. And then I rose to the surface and breathed in clean air.

Yes. Imagine it. I rose to the surface. I was conscious of the wonder of this fact. Conscious too that I was conscious. I breathed in the air. Clean, salty, sun-filtered air. I was aware that a miracle had happened. I had broken my neck for sure. It was bent forward, I couldn't straighten up. But I was alive. I moved my arms and legs. I hadn't been crippled but I had busted my neck and I had to be very, very careful. I had been immeasurably close to death and now I was alive, still among the living. I AM alive. Jesus Christ, I swore in amazement. Jesus.

When I was sure I wasn't dead – I was clutching my head half in amazement and half in pain – when I was absolutely, incredulously sure, I waded through the rocks surrounding the pool to the shore. Shock got to me quickly. I started to shiver. There was someone nearby. I called for help. Hands took hold of me and walked me to the thatched hut I had rented. Voices expressed concern.

"I'm alright," I assured them, "I just need to lie down."

I seemed to know what I was doing. I was helped to lie down. I found a position that did not induce muscular spasms. I was made comfortable. Then they left me. The babble of concern receded. After a while the shivering stopped.

It was late in the afternoon. At first there was nothing. No thoughts. Just awareness. I felt the breeze. I heard the residual muttering from the restaurant not far away. I remembered what I had done. I had done something of incomparable stupidity. I looked down again from the rock in my mind's eye. I wondered how I could ever have thought the pool was six foot deep. I could see how the curve of a rock had misled me into imagining I was looking at a diffracted image. How very silly. I smiled. It didn't matter now. I forgave myself. The best thing to do now was to lie still – as still as I could. Tomorrow I would go to the hospital. My neck was busted for sure. What a really dumb thing to do. I wiggled my toes and fingers from time to time to reassure myself. I couldn't stop the grin spreading right across my face.

I shivered a while from the shock and then the shivering went and I was wrapped in an envelope of peace and simplicity. I listened to the sea and the sky. I heard the air breathe. I saw the exquisite wonderfulness of the crimson streaks of sunset flush deep in the sky. I heard the stars sigh. I heard the beauty of the sea's rustling against the sand and I lay and listened to the voices in my heart. It took a while before I was fully aware of them. I felt no volition. I felt no desire for volition. Words arose from the depths and sank back into the depths. I listened to the words. They came and they went. I did nothing to detain them. It took a while for understanding to come – but understanding did come. I came to understand something very well. I had never understood anything quite as strongly as I now understood this new feeling. I understood that everything had become very, very simple – and I understood that I was very, very happy.

It was the most remarkable feeling, lying under the thatched roof of the beach hut, knowing that pain lurked in the back of my neck. That a spasm would hit me if I made any incautious move. From time to time I checked if I could still move my fingers or toes. I would have to be very careful. The neck was certainly broken. Any incautious move might shear the nerves that held being in place. Death was still very near but it was no longer a threat. I was at peace. Such ease and peace! All burdens had been lifted. How wonderful it was simply to be, to be alive, without doing, without thinking, without having. Yes, wonderful. The sound of the wind. The steady rhythmic surge of the surf on the sand. The lilac and orange sunset exploding in the sky timelessly.

Night came. No possibility of sleep. I sank into a dream. I became aware of myself dreaming. I pictured myself as a dream. Was I just a dream? Was it possible I could be dreamt and then forgotten? It seemed silly that now, just as I had found myself, I might die. But maybe that was when you did find yourself – as you were dying. I didn't really mind. I would be happy to sink into death if that's what was lying in wait at the other side of the night. I would not resist. Would death be that easy? Would I simply undream myself? Surely death would be harder than that? It wouldn't be a fading away. It wasn't like sleep. Or was it? I had always imagined it to be a violent wrenching, not rest and easefulness. I played with these thoughts until it occurred to me that I could feel my life force in me still very strong. Life? Could you call it life? This thing I had been leading was not a life. It wasn't living. It was drifting. It was sinking under the weight of an endless, meaningless, meaning-not-mattering existence. I tasted the failure of matter not meaning anything. But meaning was vital. Life without point – what value could it have? There had to be point: something that held it all together. What was it that made up a person, a life? Distressingly few fragments. Over the years flavours were added, subtracted. Cracks appeared. Time passed. Everything definitively finite. Was that how you made sense of a life? By adding up the facts: that endless list of accidental happenings? But what did the facts matter if they made no sense? If they could not be added up to a summation? Only meaning made sense. Only the mind could make meaning. Only the interior workings of the self had point. Imposed point. Dreams. Dreams. Dreams alone could create existence. Yes. Only dreams.

The idea that I was being dreamt amused me. Then I saw beyond the edge of the idea. I saw that only I could dream myself. I had been waiting, always waiting. I could see that now. Waiting for someone to dream me – to take hold of me and give me a ready-made dream. Now it was the end of waiting. Now was the beginning of creating. Of doing. Of imposing. Insisting. Insisting on myself. Myself most of all and the things that I myself wanted to do for the sake of doing them and for the sake of fulfilling that dark desire that came from god-knows-where to do them. Yes.

Thoughts streamed through me and I smiled at them. They did not belong to me. They had their own existence. I could touch them and make them mine if I chose to do so but otherwise they were like ducks in a shooting gallery – except no-one was shooting. The anguish had gone. The fear-sweat had gone. Only the incomparable beauty of this moment remained – the incomparable beauty of still being alive and not dead as a part of me had wanted – the part of me that had hurled the rest of me off fifteen foot of rock into three foot of water. This moment was filled with wonder at having any thoughts at all. It was wonderful to have a mind. A mind that could skip and scamper playfully among the dreams and memories and thoughts and images and ideas as if there were no difference between them all. The stars were so crisp and clear. Was there a moon? I couldn't see one. I didn't care. I had been scrubbed clean. No. Pounded clean.

Later the moon appeared somewhere to my left, a pregnant three-quarter moon. I forgot about it and then remembered it later, noting with no great surprise that it had moved. Time moved and yet time was timeless. It moved frictionlessly at its own inevitable speed. The moon was in this place. Then it was in that. If I were to die now I would die happily. But I was glad – how mightily glad it was beyond the power of words to say – to be alive. The words sang in me. Such a precious thing. Not to be wasted. Why had I not realised this before? It was such a simple truth. But it could not be reached through reason. Only blessedness. Only love could bring this happiness. To be detached from the flow and watch it pass and to let it wash through the mind for the mind to savour it and to bless it. That was all that was needed.

I lay there and knew that all I had to do to redeem myself was to choose. I chose. There and then I chose to love. And the smile I smiled cracked open my face. For I had in mind the knowledge of who it was I was in the act of choosing to love. Ah yes. Of course. Why had I not seen this before? How perfect she was for me. Not that it would necessarily be so easy. She might not agree, after all, to play her ordained part, to say yes.

And then, much later, unsought-after, dawn lightened the sky and I rose from the bed a new person. It had been so easy.

And at the hospital, miraculously, they found the neck hadn't broken – though the bouncing and banging in the bus to get there would, I thought, achieve what the dive had not. The neck was bent and I would need traction, but what did I care? I wasn't crippled. And I was alive.

And then, Stevie, later, cautiously, not quite convinced I meant what I was saying, your mother said yes.

Many years later I took her back to the rock. It took two days to track it down, I had such a vague idea of where it was. I found it eventually in the grounds of an up-market but secluded area of beach bungalows. I was disorientated. I saw a rock that might have been the rock. But it was clearly too high. No one in their right mind would have dived off the top of that. But when at last I had discounted all the other rocks, only this one was left. With a strange sense of foreboding I climbed to the top and looked down. From lower down one could see clearly how shallow the water was but from here the sun glittered off the surface and seemed to suggest greater depths – yes, this was it. I felt the fear again, a flutter in my stomach, as I contemplated just how lucky I really had been.

And I have met this rock again in other circumstances. Flying on Thai Airways, I picked up the in-flight magazine. There was a full-page advertisement for this little boutique hotel – and a picture of it, with my rock in the foreground. This little rock on a remote bay on a remote island in Thailand has a powerful genie.

Bern and I got married Chinese style. Early in the morning I arrived with my 'brothers' to kidnap the bride. The metal grille across the flat entrance was locked. Inside, Bern, your mother, sat silent while her 'sisters' loudly refused to open the door. Brothers and sisters bargained until a sum of money was agreed on – a lucky combination of threes and nines. Eventually we were let in and I kneeled on the floor to offer tea to Bern's parents and older brothers and sisters, and pour wine before the family altar. Then it was off to the registry office. Here, in a cold formal room, we were placed beside each other at a long table. Our prompts were printed with bureaucratic efficiency onto a slab of perspex that read: "I __(name)__ take you __(name)__ as my lawfully wedded wife/husband." Bern stuttered through her words and I found that she had taken me as her lawfully wedded wife... er... husband.

We travelled a lot in those first years before you arrived in our lives, Stevie. A three-month honeymoon driving around Europe. Just driving and driving. Hong Kong is a small place and to have the chance to contemplate space and distance and miles passing into the rear-view mirror was a sumptuous pleasure in itself. Bern learnt to map-read, going from near incomprehension to fine precision in a matter of days. France (where all I could remember was a smattering of Spanish), Spain (where my French returned and my Spanish deserted me), Portugal (where my Spanish was adequate), France again (where once again I had to struggle, juggling Spanish and school French), then Ireland (where the English was thick and unforgettable – but what exactly were they saying? "And what countryman are you?" a farmer asked. I admitted to being from the North: a grave mistake in a small town where there was a monument on the pier to three young men who drowned one night during the 'troubles' when they backed a truck down the pier at three one moonless morning and fell off the end into the shallow water of the river; they had been intending to land arms from a boat. Silly eejits! The farmer stalked off. I should have said I was Chinese. Then he would have welcomed me.)

Climbing the stairs in an English guesthouse, the lady taking us to our room enquired politely where we were from. I told her: Hong Kong. There was a pause and she looked at us both closely, from one to the other. Chinese face. Non-Chinese face.

"No, really," she said. "I can tell from your accent that you're not from Hong Kong."

Oh yes? My accent? Not the colour of my skin and the shape of my eyes. But Hong Kong is a multinational city with some 300,000 non-Chinese. But it's also a long way away. Filled with the mysterious vapours of the orient. How did the line go in the film *Prizzi's Honour*? "Let's forget about all this. Let's get away. Let's go to Hong Kong and change our names and disappear." Hong Kong is a gateway to the unknown. An alchemical place where people go to change identity, to change their very nature, and disappear. Didn't we know that? It was something we kept forgetting.

And then the return to England. We were both struck by the lush, rich, green beauty of the English countryside after the drab olives of Iberia. Glorious memories.

One winter, we spent three weeks on a train travelling first class around China. It was cheap then. And what magnificent trains they were, smoke-belching monsters from another age. We passed encampments of railway workers who lived in mat shed lean-tos, often decorated with a wolf pelt. On one remote station platform, high in the mountains, a man catching sight of us welcomed us to China. He thought Bern was Japanese and she was content with that, she felt so remote from her fellow countrymen.

In Taiyuan, we emerged from the railway station in the pre-dawn dark. Inevitably, a crowd gathered around us. Faces pressed close up to ours, blankly puzzled. I smiled but there was no response. None at all. We were objects of great impersonal strangeness. Then suddenly eyes connected, a face creased, a slow laugh. Others smiled. The knot of faces eased away. Taiyuan. Where the pavements were covered with an intricate tracery of frozen spittle. I felt sick to the stomach and was glad to leave.

In Hohhot, in Mongolia, we arrived after being 24 hours on the train to find that there was only one taxi in the whole city, and it had gone off with someone else. And in any case we were not expected by the travel bureau that organised all travel in those days. Dusk fell before five. Scamps in the street outside the station had Stalinesque moustaches of frozen nose drippings. It was clear they lasted all winter. I imagined the spring thaw. The railway guards took pity on us and allowed us into their cabin. With the lambswool leggings and vests that we wore, the heat from the boiler was unbearable. Outside the temperature dropped to minus twenty or more. We made telephone calls. Promises were made but nothing happened. It was five hours before the taxi returned and took us to a state guesthouse.

In Datong, a grim, dusty, frontier mining town, we took a bus to the Buddhist caves hollowed out of the cliff that ran along the bank of a wide river. On the other bank there was the black smudge of open cast coal diggings. The river was iced up and children in the distance played on it, straight from a painting by Lowry. We ventured out onto the ice a little downstream near a frozen cataract – white water indeed. As I focused the camera we heard the ice cracking. Very gingerly we returned to shore. I remember that evening walking, as dusk fell, from the bus station to the hotel down a long dusty lane two or three miles long. It seemed to go on for ever. And all around us men tramped home from their work. We were tired. I stared at the dust. We all tramped to the same beat. On, on. The steady tramp of exhausted men going home. Would we never get there? And finally we did. It was six o'clock and the kitchens were just about to close but they gave us some rice and vegetables and a bottle of dark brown ale. It was good. It was heaven. I looked at the label. Bern translated it: Two-headed Bird brand beer.

In Tibet, I remember once, but it was so typical, there was no traffic worth speaking of as we started to cross a road. Bern took my arm in hers to guide us both safely across. She had an obsessive concern. How strange that this memory should stand out so clearly against the intense images of large men, large women – radiating size in many dimensions – dressed in shaggy yak skins

– with nothing underneath, as we discovered when one drunken woman sprawled into a gutter – and the pervasive thick smell of rancid butter. These people radiated strange unnerving energies that vibrated in the still, thin, dry air that foreshortened everything so that it seemed everything was just there – right there so that one could just reach out and grasp it. The smooth hills along all sides of the valley looked five hundred feet high, perhaps, not the three thousand they really were. The Potala, that seems so grand and tall in the photographs, is dwarfed by these surrounding slopes which mark the edge of the surrounding Tibetan plateau. And yet, in the front of my mind, I have this image of Bern collecting me by the arm to shepherd me to the safety of the far side of the road. Always looking after other people.

In a stone village in southwest China, I have a picture of Bern and myself under siege from fifty to a hundred girls, all dressed in the local native costume of their tribal minority, waving embroidered shoes, wanting to sell them. Bern had a small curio shop in those days and was stocking up. An hour before, we had passed the word to a local shopkeeper that we were in the market for embroidered goods. He had told us to return after an hour. When we did so we found dozens of girls waiting for us. They mobbed us, waving their embroidered cotton shoes in the air, their very own work, desperate that we might not want them, desperate for the currency. Bern bought every single pair. I don't think she was ever happier than at that moment.

The flitter of random memories. We travelled well together.

At that time we lived in a small flat at the top of a hill on a small island, an hour by ferry from the main island of Hong Kong. It is a very small island. With recent reclamations it is almost exactly one square mile. Two largish headlands of rotten granite joined by a wasp waist of a sand bar. Geographers call this type of island a tombolo. It is perhaps three hundred paces across at the thinnest point. The shape of it is like a dog, if you look at it in a certain way, or maybe a knotted root of ginger. The sandbar has been concreted over and built upon. This is the village where some thirty, forty or even fifty thousand people live, no-one has been able to agree on the precise figure. Three-storey blocks line the two alleys that run the length of the strip. On the south side of the sandbar, six hundred or so trawlers, fishing junks, shrimpers, sampans, water boats, grain junks, short-haul cargo boats and fibre-glass skips occupy the waters of the harbour area. On the north side is the island's main beach which looks on to the south side of Hong Kong Island – a scatter of lights on a clear night – and beyond it the furnace of the blazing city, alive with evening energies. Sometimes, late in the evening we watched it with a kind of awe. But mostly we faced the other way, looking across the inky harbour to the silent dark shapes of the mountains on the neighbouring island of Lantau, slopes that faded away in shades of grey.

The flat, one of four in the block, stood just below the peak of one of the two hills on the island, overlooking some vegetable plots. One day, instead of going down to the market, I decided to buy directly from the farmer.

"How much do you want?" he asked. We stood facing each other surrounded by the vegetables in the field grappling with this question of quantity.

"A catty," I suggested tentatively, aware of the stupidity of talking weight when we had nothing to weigh them in. We laughed.

"OK, two dollars worth."

My Cantonese was up to that. The farmer nodded and started laying the white cabbage along his arm. From wrist to elbow one dollar, from elbow to shoulder two dollars. For two dollars I got an arm's length of Chinese greens.

To the left of the house was the wide bay of the harbour. To the right, rocks fell down to the open sea a stone's throw away. We shared the nights with the croakings of a hundred frogs, rich bellowings like cows' mooings. I loved these frog sounds, each burping like bubbles bursting, that greeted us as we came home in the evening. At night it was sometimes too tiresome to go out into the town at the bottom of the hill. We stayed where we were and closed out the world. Our closest friends were insects and trees. Spiders weaved their cobwebs unmolested, skinks darted out from the wardrobe. Blue tailed skinks – lizards that looked as if they had been designed by Bugatti. They skittered around the room on electric nerves. Sometimes a tail was missing, leaving a glistening red lump. Within a week the tail had grown back. Cicadas grated their legs together in sudden frenzies of sound. In the drains and cracks around the house lived armoured centipedes up to ten inches long. In the grass there were snakes. We were not alone in our solitude.

They were happy times, times of deep contentment and a strange, disquieting need to escape. I recognise this only now, looking back, there were deep currents of energy that felt constrained. And as I look back at this companionable, contented time, I guess Bern too was escaping along her own tracks of wood and stone. Dear Stevie, I loved your mother and she loved me. These are truths that I know absolutely. But perhaps there was – in me, in her – at the centre, a hard core that could not be dissolved in the acid of love. And, anyway, love isn't all there is to it. There's more. And did we leak away from each other slowly, a slow steady drip-drip-drip of soul and spirit and heart and being? So very slowly we didn't notice it? So slowly that even if we had seen it we wouldn't have thought it mattered? Is that what happened? It's hard to think of it. But then of course the drip, if there was a drip, was small and the reservoir of feeling was deep.

And life, in any case, means friction and people are different, grow differently, react differently. These are simple everyday truths.

And then, Stevie, there was you. A seed planted in the very heart-soil of our lives.

I knew it before she did. I knew the firming of the breast meant more than temporary hormonal dysfunction. I knew what the delay in the menstrual flow must mean but she was confused. She had had the signs before. The signs had been wrong. This time was different. The days passed and the subtle ballooning of her breasts continued. I grew more certain. But she was confused. There had been a slight flow of blood at the proper time and again a few weeks later and again and again, each time after we had made love.

When it was confirmed she said we'd have to stop for a couple of months. It could be dangerous. How did I feel about it? There I was, excluded from the body I loved for the sake of the usurper. I thought of the burden, the irritations, the complications of it all. But that mood didn't last long. I became affectionate of the little abstraction that daily grew bigger and bigger. You. But I didn't know it then. I felt this nameless fruit of love ripen under the palm of my hand; saw it swell. Her nipples stuck out straight as if at attention. We lay in bed holding hands and contemplating this mysterious child that had chosen to be ours – or had it been chosen for us by some unseen fate? Was it that aeons of karma were meeting at this intersection of fate and time? Magical and mysterious being. What were we going to do with you? What were you going to do to us?

We understood a truth. The future had arrived. And what we saw as the future would always be your continuous present.

And looking back, Stevie, as I sometimes do, I feel a kind of horror rise up in me. If we had known then. If we had suspected. If we had had tests. And such tests! Plunging a huge needle into the amniotic sac and drawing out some of the fluid that protected you from the bumps of the world. And analysing the cells of your foetal excretions. With a one to two percent chance of aborting you. If we had done that, then we would never have known you. That thought scares me to the depth of my soul. If I had never known you, why then, I would never have become the me I am today.

We become encrusted with the sediments that life throws at us. They become impacted. Layer is laid upon layer. We adapt ourselves. We change. What would happen if these ancient crusts were peeled away? It hardly bears thinking of. We only have the life we are given. It is folly to sit and dream and wish that things could be different, that we could be given different lives. This is a hard, unpleasant truth. But Stevie, when you were with us, thankfully, you were not aware that there were other putative lives that might have been embraced if only things were just a little different. In the light of your own life this thought takes on a little poignancy.

And the snakes were a worry, the poisonous centipedes for some reason plaguing only the other half of the building and leaving us alone. Mainly, they were harmless rat snakes but more and more, recently, we had seen the small, nearly invisible, bright emerald bamboo snakes – so like the thin leaves of certain trees you had to peer closely to make sure. One night, bathed in bright moonlight, Bern and I sauntered up the path, past the frog pond, up a sudden steep incline, along the cracked concrete path. The harbour put-putted below with the coughing of sampan engines.

"We've just passed a snake," Bern said.

"No, it's just a crack in the path."

"It's a snake."

"Don't be silly. It's just a crack."

We both stared down. I had a torch in a bag and dragged it out. There in the beam was a young bamboo snake, sitting perfectly still, staring into the light. We had walked one on either side of it. If we had stood on it, it would surely have retaliated. The bamboo is one of the more poisonous of the local snakes. Bern became quite proficient in pouring boiling water over them when they came too close to the house. They jerked and shivered in their frantic death dance throes.

A friend said: "Some people say a pregnant woman mustn't harm any living being in case the spirit of the animal comes and punishes the baby."

Is that what happened, Stevie? Did the snake spirit...? I don't even know how to finish the thought. I know the friend wishes now she had bitten her tongue. But how can a curse turn out a blessing? I'm sorry. Stevie, you're right. A blessing to who? It wasn't fair on you. Not fair at all. But what has fairness got to do with it in the end?

But as your mother grew heavier, the walk up the hill grew more tiring. We had to move. We took a flat in the village and moved down. I kept the old flat as an office, where I stayed all alone during the day, except for the company of the family of blue-tailed skinks: Every spring they emerged from the nest they had made in some long-forgotten box in one of the cupboards I no longer wanted to open. All summer they skittered and scootered around. Years came and went but we never really became friends, though there came a time when they would tolerate me and no longer react with hair-trigger speed to my slightest movement. I wrote my books and felt secure.

Dear Stevie, your mother took to pregnancy like a rosy red flower to the ripening sun. And then, one day, you arrived. And you were going to be called Patrick if you were a boy and Stevie if you were a girl. Stevie. Not so much after the poet Stevie Smith as because of her. It was a name that conjured up a rugged tomboyishness that I approved of.

Oh Stevie. How little I knew then.

One afternoon, having just got home from having done the

shopping, Bernadette felt the cramps coming on so we walked down to the ferry and took the next boat in to Hong Kong. The white three-deck ferry sailed out of the small bay of the island and headed for the western entrance to Hong Kong harbour. It was a cold day in February.

Bern's waters broke ten minutes before we docked at the pier. We managed to get a taxi and with a delightful quiver of near panic we drove to the hospital. No-one was willing to say how long it would be. The idea of spending long hours on a wooden bench, perhaps all night, only to have to be supportive all the next day did not appeal. There was only an even chance that I would be able to observe the birth – the delivery room was a double one and there might easily be another birth that night. And now that it came to the point I felt a certain queasiness about the prospect of blood and pain and feeling useless and in the way. So I left Bern to it, left her to cope on her own with the business of giving birth to you.

The next morning, shortly after seven, I arrived at the hospital to be informed it was all over. A girl had been born at three o'clock. So I crept to Bern's bed and kissed her and then tip-toed away.

The past is a distant country. Some days are clear. Some days are wrapped in obscuring fogs.

She called me mid-morning and said the doctor wanted to talk to us both. The doctor? A formality no doubt. I gave it no thought. But Bern's family were all there. They could smell danger a mile away. A doctor wanted to say something...?

It was three o'clock in the afternoon of the very first day of your existence. The doctor had said he wanted to talk to us and there we were. Bern was worried but I didn't give it a thought. I still hadn't seen you. Not really. You had been pointed out to me through a window. There you were in the babies' room. Which one? Small curled-up blobby faces. How could you tell one from another? And why was it in there anyway? It. It was a public hospital that didn't see why it should have to amend its systems for the individual patient.

The doctor arrived and we went into a side room.

"The first thing I have to tell you is good news. She is a healthy girl."

We nodded and squeezed hands.

"Unfortunately, I also have some bad news. It seems she has Down's syndrome."

What?

"What does this mean? It means she will be slow. She will grow up to be physically weak and she will be a slow learner. Her intelligence may be about half a normal person's intelligence. I am sorry to tell you this but it is better that you know sooner than later."

I had only the vaguest understanding of what this Down's syndrome was.

"All you can do is take her home and love her. She will be very loving and happy."

We were lost. This first baby of our happiness. Our minds froze. We heard the words, we recorded them but they fell into a deep well of horror. Perhaps, he saw the shock on our faces. He wanted to lessen the blow.

"Now, at the moment this is just a suspicion. It is not one

hundred per cent certain. But in fact she has some of the signs. But we won't know until we have done some cell tests. We will arrange for you to have genetic counselling."

"Is it something we have done?" Bern asked.

"No. Don't blame yourself. It was nothing you did."

"How did this happen?"

"It's not your fault. No-one is to blame. It is something that happens at random. One in seven to eight hundred babies. Don't blame yourself."

Mind blank. Stomach empty and sticky with shock. Stunned, vacant, annihilated. I wanted to comfort Bern who had gone through the pain of birth for this... this further pain. I hugged her as warmly as I could without hurting her. Then we asked the nurse to bring the baby in – and then suddenly there you were.

Up till then it had all been so sudden and so abstract. I looked at this poor lump of flesh – yes, you, Stevie – feeling so sad for it to have its life's chances blasted so absolutely so early on. And I felt a sudden, very powerful sense of possession. This was my baby and something was wrong with it... her... you. The baby, this baby, was utterly vulnerable and defenceless. It was up to me to fight for it. And it, she, you, looked cute – in fact it – she, you – looked quite normal to me.

One minute you were simply an idea. A something that had gone wrong. An incomprehension. The next minute you were there and as I looked at you all bound up in the white cotton towelling, your face orangey pink and soft, I saw... I felt... There was a sudden rush of feelings and understandings.

First you were just a little baby. You were our little baby. God damn it! You were my daughter. And you weren't a problem. You weren't our problem. You were a small, fragile human being and already you had the burden of this problem and who was going to help you if I didn't help you? And God damn it! I was going to help you. I was going to do everything in my power to help you through this problem – whatever that meant. And... and... I fell in love with you completely. In a moment. Just like that. I felt some power in me reach out and embrace you and become one with you. In short we bonded. I felt it as a physical act. It seemed so unfair that you were so new and you had to bear this thing, this pain, this difference, whatever it was. Oh and you were so beautiful.

There was a moment the next day, as I walked to the hospital, when a dark spectral thought loomed in on me. This thought spoke to me something like this: "Your life is a failure. You're amounting to nothing. Your marriage frankly is in a mess. You have no dreams. The wisps of desire that you call ambition have led you into a cul-de-sac. And now this. A malformed baby. Another failure. God's... fate's... sign to you that your life is a swamp of failure. This is just one more failure and it will trap you in your continuing failure for how can you escape this one? A pillow over the face?"

I remember reaching my hand out and pushing this thought away from me hard. I saw the disease in the thought. I knew I had to choose. I chose to see her, it, you, as a person with a problem, not a problem with a face. I chose to see it as her, your, problem not mine. I was part of the solution, not a part of the problem.

And again another question loomed in on me:

"Why? Why me?"

And I saw that this too was an unhealthy question. A question that oozed the viscous jelly of self-pity. And I saw the answer that rang true. If it could happen to anyone, it could happen to me. The right question was not 'why me?' but 'why not me?'

But there was a pain, a real physical pain in my chest, a knot of unreleased emotions – a blood blister of bruised expectation. It was to stay there, over the heart, for a month to six weeks. And Bern? She didn't speak of her feelings and I didn't ask her. Each of us was caught up with the intensity of our own private response.

And the pillow over the face? Was that the right solution? I contemplated it, Stevie. I did. And I decided I would do it. But I would do it only on one condition: I would do it only if you could not live a life that was bearable to you. If life weren't worth living for you, I would do it. But I wouldn't do it for myself. Somehow that seemed to dispose of the question for I never ever contemplated it again as a possibility.

On the third day it came to me that there must be someone we could talk to. That we didn't need to sit around and wait for the doctors to make the next move. I honestly didn't know what sort of help there might be out there – but there had to be someone we could talk to. I phoned the Community Advice Bureau who gave me the number of a child development centre. I phoned up rehearsing in my mind what I was going to say. I was going to tell her the problem and ask her what sort of help there might be for Stevie. Very simple. Very matter of fact. A woman answered and I went through the details. There was a pause at the other end and then this immensely warm and kind voice embraced me with sympathy: "And how are you feeling?" – that subtle intimate focus of stress on 'you' – and the tears exploded down my face and my mouth opened in voiceless agony. "How are you coping?" she asked and I guess there was about five minutes of silence while I arranged my features and regained control of my voice.

That first week was a time of great pain for me. I felt it literally as a great weight in my chest. I didn't know what to say to the people who came up to congratulate me. I was very confused and I suppose everybody did get the message very clearly that not all was well. Hope came and went, a wild hope that the doctor was wrong. I kept trying not to hope but it was difficult. I knew hope was just getting in the way, interfering with the coming to terms with it all process.

I remember thinking that 'Stevie' was a name I had associated with a lively, active, tomboyish girl – and you were definitely not going to be that girl. Perhaps I should take the name back and give you another name, so I could keep 'Stevie' for the next one – if there was a next one. But that seemed to be very wrong. I felt I couldn't steal this name back. I had already mentally given it to you. To have your name stolen back seemed to me to be very wrong. So Stevie you became. I remember a friend saying what a nice name it was and how she could imagine you in twenty years' time picking up the phone and saying: "Hi. This is Stevie Chamberlain." And it seemed so smart. And I bit my tongue and stopped myself telling her that it was never going to be like that.

"Well, you can change it if you want," Bern said, as always pragmatic. Being Chinese, changing one's name to fit a new circumstance was in any case the thing to do. But it seemed very wrong somehow. So much identity is tied up in names. You had been born with so many problems. To have your name taken away too would be to add a further insult. So Stevie you remained. And I would never have forgiven myself if I had changed it. It would have remained a subtle reproach to the end. Even up to now.

It was ten days before you were to come out of hospital. For those ten days I was caught permanently off balance.

"How's Bern?" friends asked. "How's the baby?"

"Oh fine. Fine."

I fielded congratulations with a heavy heart because I didn't want to tell anyone until they saw you. I wanted them to see you first. Then I would tell them. But Bern didn't want to tell anyone anything. She wanted to hug the pain close to herself and hide. I knew this was wrong. I knew this was not something we could negotiate.

And the first person we told put it all into perspective. We were on the ferry heading back to the island. We found ourselves sitting next to Joan, a woman we knew vaguely who had been fighting cancer for a year or so. She told us she had just learnt it had come back. It was inoperable. She had had a hard life and she was bitter it was about to end soon. I told her about you, Stevie. This woman looked at you lying in your wicker basket with its red gingham border and then she looked at us.

"Well, she's healthy, isn't she?"

"Yes."

"And she's happy?"

"Yes."

"And you love her?"

"Yes."

"Well then? What's the problem?"

And compared with her problem it was of course no problem.

And when we got to the island we found our friends seated at a streetside bar and I pushed Bern up the steps towards them.

"Here she is," I said.

Naturally they were all happy to make a fuss.

"Now, poor Stevie has a problem..."

And it was a relief to say the words.

Poor Bern. She really did not want it said but it had to be said, for all our sanity.

We were very lucky. Every one of our relatives and friends made a great point of expressing their strong support. We felt lost and very vulnerable with this new responsibility but we had this support – and this was extremely important for our sanity and relationship. I remember wondering how my mother would take the news. I took photos of you and sent them with the letter. You were a person with a problem, not a problem personified. Later, she said to us: "I woke up one morning and I thought: that's strange. We haven't heard from Jonathan. I wonder if anything's wrong with the baby. Well, if something is wrong, I hope it's Down's syndrome because they're so happy and loving."

Over the next two weeks we both went around as if shell-shocked. I remember us both sitting wordlessly, stunned, in the sitting room with this little baby, you, in your cot. Some struggle for comprehension was going on. Somehow we knew we had to put in the foundations of how life was going to be. Where were we to start? But then slowly, as you grew, so too did we.

And later I wrote something to try and capture the moment.

The Baby

The baby was a one in 700 chance. The sort of chance you'd bet heavily on. Why not? 699 times you win. 699 for to one against. Good odds.

We got the one in 700 slot. The jackpot. Genetic defect. A baby with faulty wiring. What does that mean? In her case it meant having more genes than you or me. More genes than she could deal with. She had a built-in jamming device. Some of the messages got scrambled. Not many, really. Who knows how many? Scrambled. Incoherent. Well, not exactly incoherent. Smudged. Again, not entirely. A certain confusion – not more.

Poor wee being! It hurt to be lumbered with this bag of flesh and bad circuit design. A drooling idiot? A vegetable? The awful fear. The heavy burden of joy's ashes lying leaden in the breast. She only an idea. Poor sod. Lost in a wizardry of improbable figures and awkward expertises. You want figures? One in seven pregnancies end in miscarriage. One in two miscarriages involve babies with faulty wiring (poor wee dears). Most babies with faulty wiring short-circuit. One in 300 don't. They're strong. They make it. Beautiful. And she being brand new and you know consequently a little floppy and unsure we were careful of her. And the weight in the breast that lay so heavily, puddingly, dissolved itself in the growing delight we had in her who was ours – who was flawed and who was ours. And she became a person more than we ever expected. Her bright eyes quivered as she explored the volumes of space around her, in her sight paths she found wonders where we saw nothing. Wonderful. Her eyes danced choreographies of wonder. Such wonder and delight at this new thing called seeing.

We were left holding the baby. It can hit you bad. It hit us so hard we didn't know what to do. Love. We had never expected that. Neither the two things. The flawed being (the perfect being with the flawed electrics) and the love that poured out of us and slopped all over her until she nearly drowned in it.

Floppy. Yes. I can still feel the soft, flaccid pressure of your body moulded to my shoulder. I liked to lie on the bed with you on my stomach. Your arms were by your side and you liked to flex yourself like a penguin – like a sky-diver – as you arched your neck round to observe the room around you: volumes of space, choreographies of wonder.

Oh Stevie. If only we could have stayed there in that moment for ever. Fly away Stevie, I said to you. And we hugged and you were so tiny in my arms.

A stray memory. I remember being very aware that the only hair you had was a long feathery plume that ran punk style down the centre of your scalp. I was terrified that this was part of the syndrome. That you were always going to look like that. What did I know? Some friends suggested dyeing it green and purple. I may have smiled weakly at the idea but a small voice inside me shrieked with horror. It was the terrible fear that you would be some kind of freak. I did not even think to think what kind of freak. It was the shadow of a shadow of an idea at the very edge of consciousness. I could not name it. I couldn't turn to look it straight in the eye.

But as long as you looked like a relatively normal little baby I was all right. It was the seed of the threat of what you might turn into that caused me to pause. I didn't know then what a beautiful little girl you were going to become.

Then I did something that it took your mother a long time to forgive me for. You were just six weeks old and she, like me, was struggling to comprehend what had happened to us. I left the two of you and went on a two-and-a-half week cycling trip around Hainan Island. I knew Bern was unhappy about it. Yes, I should have been there for her. But I needed some space. I needed to escape from the oppression of feeling. I needed to work something out of my system in a hard, physical, brutal way. Yes, yes. Excuses, excuses.

I have two images that have stayed with me from the trip.

On the third day, we set off from the coast to a town in the centre of the island. It was going to be a long day, the longest of the trip at 110 kilometres. But we weren't too worried. The roads had been good so far, surprisingly good. We had been putting in good mileage. We felt good. But, in retrospect, it might have been better to have stopped and rested. But the truth was the town we had spent the second night in was not so interesting and we were there to do some serious cycling.

About a mile out of town the road of cement and tarmac ended.

It soon became clear that this was no aberration. Soon the dirt road began to climb. It was hot. We began to worry that we hadn't brought enough water.

"We'll pick up some more at the first place we come to," Iain said. Iain was our tour leader.

It wasn't all uphill. The terrain undulated but the general tendency was upwards. When we came to the downhill stretches it was fun at first. We would careen down the slopes trying to pick up speed for the next uphill stretch. But we soon found that at the bottom of the hill the sand had always settled several inches thick so that it was all we could do to stop ourselves skidding and toppling over. The bags we were carrying gave us ballast and we soon got the hang of it.

All morning we climbed wearily up hills and then freewheeled down the other side. We passed no villages or roadside shops. There was no traffic to speak of. We soon got tired of the sight of rubber trees. Inevitably our water gave out. The sun glared in a cloudless sky. Then, around about twelve, I caught sight of two rubber tappers. With sign language I tried to get some idea from them as to how far we were from the next village. They seemed to indicate it was two or three hills away, maybe twenty minutes. On we went, grinding up unforgiving slopes. Sun glinted off the quartz on the road and diffracted through the pasty, salty, beads of sweat that bathed the face. We climbed the first three hills and then the next three and the three after that. On and on. It was getting serious now. We had no choice but to keep going. The only way to deal with it was to become numb. Just keep going. Just this hill. Just this one. Just one more to go. OK. Just one more to go. One more. Maybe this one. Just keep pedalling. Come on. Focusing on the tyre crunching into the sand.

And then, around about two o'clock, we came over the brow of a hill and there it was. A dozen buildings. We headed straight for the general store. I drank eighteen glasses of chemical-flavoured ice water one after the other. And we still had another fifty kilometres to go. We eventually arrived at the next town at ten o'clock in the evening.

That day's cycling taught me something. Perseverance.

My second memory was of an incident that occurred towards the end of the trip. We were tired and looking forward to the end. We had got into a comfortable rhythm and feeling good about the pace we were setting for ourselves. The roads were good and the scenery was unspectacular: water-buffaloes in paddy fields, coconut palms and farmers protecting themselves from the occasional showers with straw coverings and conical rattan hats, very much as you can see them in Japanese woodcuts from a hundred years ago. From time to time I glanced up but most of the time I was content to focus on the road immediately ahead and the white line that ran down the middle of the road. We came to a town that stretched itself along both sides of the road. Just two long strings of houses. It was the middle of the day and no-one was about. We barely slowed down. We were strong now and easy in the saddle, comfortable with our speed. Ahead we could see the end of the town and the large banyan that every town in China had, the spirit tree. It barely registered. Every village had a pond. Every village had its tree. Eyes looking down at the road for potholes, quick sweep to check the road ahead. No traffic. No black pigs slumped in our way. Good. Eyes down again scanning the next twenty yards or so. Quick check again. Strange how...? The thought ending before it began. What? Surely, it can't be. Suddenly...

In retrospect you could see how it would have happened. The district planners had drawn the route of the road. It was to go here, like this, straight as an arrow. But the town's people would have been equally adamant. No-one cuts down our spirit tree. And so they both won. The road remained straight as an arrow and the tree still stood where it always had, though now it occupied the entire right lane of the road. The white lines marking the centre of the road went over its roots. Good business for the local garage.

We had to swerve sharply across the road to avoid crashing straight into it.

Is there a moral there, Stevie? We're cruising down a long straight road. We think we know where we're going. We think we can see ahead into the future and the view is clear. But if we're not careful we can smash straight into a tree that's standing where we never expected it to. The road of life. The tree of fate.

Another memory. This too is about fate. The small zoo was virtually deserted and the animals sweated in the midday sun. A Tibetan bear sat slumped, dazed in its own stink of piss. Apart from me there were only three other visitors. I noticed that they were standing rapt, staring into one of the exhibits. They just stood there, motionless. Clearly something of interest. I ambled over to see what it was. Then I saw it and I too stared at this scenario, as good as anything by Hitchcock. In the concrete box, separated from us by a glass window, lay two Burmese pythons. They lay in shallow troughs coiled in lengths. From time to time a ripple would flow like a wave down the length of the snake. There was a third animal in the compartment, a small puppy, totally unaware that he was lunch. It is well-known that pythons will only eat live food. This was it. But the pup did not know this. It had no inherited sense that snakes were dangerous. It snuffled and poked with curious interest where it could. And sometime, one of the two snakes was going to wake from its slumber and decide it was hungry. And that's what kept us all transfixed staring through the glass. We're all like that puppy, Stevie, how little we know of the perils that lie in store for us.

One last memory, apropos of nothing. We were on the ship taking us back to Hong Kong, except that our crisp new direct ferry to Hong Kong had broken down and instead we were on the hell-ship to Guangzhou. The crew occupied the first class quarters and the passengers, us, were in the bilges. Ever since then I have carried with me the concept of the China ferryboat category of organisation – the organisation that is run for the benefit of the staff, the crew.

The ship had just entered the Pearl River estuary. Hong Kong was to the right, Macau to the left and we still had another half day ahead of us as the ship ploughed steadily on. Les, a financial journalist, had a small portable radio that he was fiddling with. We had been out of touch with the world for eighteen days now. What had been happening in the world? He looked at me in some bemusement.

"I don't know what the hell has happened while we've been away," he said, "but something has wiped out a third of the Russian wheat harvest."

We were possibly the last people on earth to hear about Chernobyl.

But your mother got her revenge. Some mornings she would tell me that it was my turn to look after you and she would disappear for the day. These were days of awful terror. To be alone and responsible for a little baby when you know nothing about little babies...! Panic.

The doctor in the genetic counselling unit took us through the stigmata of Down's syndrome. He showed us how your eyes were at a slightly higher angle than normal. How the gap between your thumb and the other fingers was larger than normal. He looked at the creases of the hand. It is common for this to be just a single crease. But Stevie, your hand creases were little different from mine or Bern's. Then the doctor opened his own hand. He had just a single crease himself, typical in Down's syndrome. He laughed.

There was no doubt that you had Down's syndrome. The slides were clear. Then we learnt that there are three kinds of Down's syndrome. Yours was the common kind, whose cause is unknown and which occurs with random regularity, somewhere between one in 700 to 1,000.

And what was Down's? The doctor drew pictures showing how the normal cell of 46 chromosomes, organised in 23 numbered pairs, should divide into two other cells of 46 chromosomes. He showed how this was different in the case of Down's syndrome. Here the cell divided into a cell containing 45 chromosomes and a cell containing 47. The cell with 45 chromosomes died but in the case of Down's, when the extra chromosome belonged to chromosome pair 21, the cell remained viable and continued to subdivide with each subsequent cell containing 47 chromosomes. The extra chromosome gives out genetic messages that blur the impact of the messages given out by the other two chromosomes. Pair 21 is not a very important pair so the impact of the blurring is not necessarily life threatening. But it affects the muscles – less tone; the immune system – much weaker; the heart – great likelihood of heart defects; eyesight, hearing, physique, mental functioning and on and on. Oh Stevie! But as long as you had a happy and satisfying life.

We learnt that there was a rare form of Down's syndrome where not every cell in the body contained 47 chromosomes. In this case, the flawed cell division occurred slightly later than the first. This meant some of the tissues had Down's syndrome characteristics and some had normal characteristics. The muscle could be Down's-type tissue while the bones might be made of 46 chromosome tissue – normal tissue. But 'normal' covers a wide range. In the area of intelligence, normality ranges from IQ 70 to 130, from fairly slow to reasonably bright. For of course, the nervous system might be housed in a body that looked Down's but was composed of 46 chromosome tissue. The logic of this fact meant that it was theoretically possible for someone with Down's syndrome to go to university and even go on to become a professor of Medicine – unlikely, indeed highly improbable, but possible. Of course, this didn't apply to you, Stevie, but somehow I was comforted by the technical complexities of your condition. Something was known about it. I could read up about it. I could gain some sort of control over our new fate.

At first everything seemed fine. We were fortunate in finding two centres where we were taught exercises and activities that were designed to help you learn the skills you needed to learn, that every 'normal' baby learnt as a matter of course: rolling over, sitting up, holding your head straight. We were taught to move your leg up so that the knee bent and then to push the leg over so that the body would follow; taught to pull you gently to a sitting position and other exercises that seemed sensible. It was going to be OK. We just had to get used to the fact that you were different. You would progress at your own speed. And that's all there was to it. So we thought. We met other parents in our position. It seemed, on the whole, we could console ourselves that you weren't the worst affected baby.

And you brought us closer together and strengthened our love. About other things there were some differences. About you there were none.

'Early intervention'. That was the name of the game. The more you do with the child, the better it will progress, hopefully. Oh Stevie, what a strange world it is. Some years later, at a conference on mental retardation, a doctor was drafted in at short notice to talk about 'early intervention'. She had almost finished her presentation when I realised what the problem was: in the medical world, the conjunction of mental handicap and early intervention meant only one thing: abortion. Oh dear. One phrase, two meanings, as Deng Xiaoping might have put it.

Dear Stevie, you seemed to progress so well. We felt you were going to be OK, you were going to be mildly retarded, maybe even borderline. One of the pieces of information I was very happy to come across in the British Down's Syndrome Association's magazine was the fact that some children with Down's Syndrome had IQs above 70. This meant to me that one could not therefore automatically label them 'mentally handicapped' or whatever the correct term was. All of which, in turn, meant it was worth fighting and giving you as much stimulation as we could. Let's face it. It was therapy for us too. Who knew what the future held? For a few months I was excited about this new world we were discovering.

You were an exciting new adventure.

Oh dear me, Stevie. The linguistic problems were something else. What after all was the correct term? And what about this insistence on correctness and the righteous anger that seemed so much a part of the this new world we were travelling through.

Over the months and years that followed I read what I could to understand what I could, in a general sort of way, so that I might know something of the parameters of the discussions of the world of medicine, of psychology, of child development as they affected you. I found a world of learning and I found deep streams of passion. And I found the problem of names.

There were, for example, those who insisted that there was nothing 'mentally' wrong with children like you and that therefore to say you were 'mentally handicapped' was wrong. (This was the new voice; the old voice still spoke of 'idiots' and 'morons' as if these were acceptable scientific terms – I had some sympathy with this abrasive new voice). Some suggested that the term 'intellectually disabled' was more appropriate. Personally, I always found this confusing. Both 'mentally' and 'intellectually' cover a similar territory of meaning but it seemed to me that 'intellectually' covers a more closely focused sense, something more restricted to rational thought. It didn't seem to me that, as yet, we knew enough about the psychology of the many conditions and causes of what for better or worse I choose to call mental handicaps to narrow our focus like this usefully. The other term, 'disability', to me suggested a complete – or near complete – inability to do something; a much more negative perception than that of handicap, which merely suggests – to me at least – a degree of difficulty.

Then there were those who thought the term 'impaired' sounded better, or was truer to the thing itself.

The distinction between these three words was once explained to me thus: A man who has had a leg amputated has a serious impairment that prevents him from doing many things, so the level of disability is great, but if he makes a living as an accountant and lives at home the level of handicap is small. Similarly, another man may have a slight impairment, a blister on a toe for example, that does not prevent very much activity, so again the level of disability is low. But if one of his jobs is to walk ten miles to fetch water which he is now prevented from doing, it amounts to a major handicap.

In the end, I came to the conclusion that it was simply a matter of labels. Whatever label we used, if applied to an area viewed with ignorance and suspicion by the average uninvolved person, would acquire a negative tone.

Labels that help us usefully isolate a group of people for some positive, appropriate and focused intervention are good. Labels that focus simply on negative features for the purposes of rejection or localised abuse are bad. All else is hair-splitting.

Of course, the real objection to the use of 'mentally' is its association with mental illness and the mental asylum. Certainly, too few people are aware of the distinction between mental illness and mental handicap. For the average uninformed person, it is easy to confuse them. Both seem to refer to 'something wrong with mental functions'. However, these terms refer to quite different problems as is immediately obvious as soon as it is explained.[1]

Oh Stevie. Were you Impaired? Disabled? Handicapped?

---

[1] *Mental illness* refers to the area of emotional or psychological malfunctioning – neurotic or psychotic or just sheer awful collapse of the inner being that can affect anyone and which is curable, at least in theory, either through psychological therapy or medication or the passage of time or some internal chemical click. This is a medical problem requiring the intervention of doctors and nurses. The mentally ill may need to be segregated from normal society for their own safety, or because they are a danger to others. They are, generally speaking, adults. Issues affecting the mentally ill are mental health issues. But journalists and newspapers, it seems, cannot be educated out of the convenience this term has to apply to the handicapped.

Mental handicap, on the other hand, should perhaps be better described as developmental retardation. It is a term that applies to children and adults whose level of intelligence is sub-average and whose rate of learning is slower. It is almost always a permanent condition that cannot be cured. People with mental handicaps are not 'ill', they are, generally speaking, perfectly healthy. They may have genetic conditions but these cannot be treated with medications. They don't need doctors and nurses – except, when like you or me, they are ill. People with mental handicaps need the intervention of developmental psychologists and special education teachers, not doctors or drugs. People with mental handicaps need to be integrated into normal society, not separated from it. Most mentally handicapped – over half – are children. They are rarely dangerous. Issues affecting this population are generally discussed under the headings of special education or rehabilitation.

Retarded? Which word was truer to the way you were? Perhaps the best answer is to use the euphemism 'special'.

Yes, Stevie, you were special. You were a special little Down's baby. And in saying this I am treading on other sensitive toes. I have no objection to saying "she's a Down's kid". Yes, 'a kid with Down's' is arguably better – not so defining: the condition is an attribute, not the core, of being. Yes, but let's not be too purist. We go around defining people all the time: the blonde, the black guy, the old fellow – the part is taken to identify the whole. Is this so bad? Do we really want to say the person with black skin, the man with old age? (The man of old age? Even our grammar rebels against the construction). Let's get real. Let's not go to war over it.

And Down's at least sounds huggable (to me, Stevie, because of you. I always want to hug you. Even now when you're not here to be hugged I close my eyes and wrap my arms around a volume of space and pretend you're in it and that I can feel your weight) – though one person asked me in some confusion: "Why do you call it Down Syndrome? It sounds so depressing. Why don't you call it Up Syndrome instead?" Why not indeed? [2]

---

[2] The pedestrian answer, of course, is that the syndrome was named after a certain Dr Down, who was the first to isolate – and, more importantly, to describe in the medical press – the group as a coherent one with identifiable characteristics. However, the truth is, Dr Down misunderstood what he had found and thought that the condition represented some form of ethnic degeneration from the high European racial level to the lower 'Mongolian' level. Behind this thinking was a racial Darwinism first put forward by one Robert Chambers who, in 1844, wrote: "Our brain goes through the various stages of a fish's, a reptile's and a mammifer's brain

But I think it was the Olmecs who got it right. Two thousand years ago they lived in what is now southern Mexico. They saw that people like you Stevie were very special, rare and good humoured, happy and loving. These people must therefore, the Olmecs reasoned, be special ambassadors from heaven. They carved stone sculptures to honour you.

From very early on, I came to think of you, Stevie, as a special ambassador from Heaven.

You were three months old when the doctors first heard the slight echo in your heart that we all were hoping they wouldn't hear. It was very slight, they said. Maybe it was small enough to self-correct.

We waited in cold wide hospital corridors that cried out for benches for people to sit on, while we waited for the doctors to get to us. Finally, the extraordinary technology that enabled us to see inside your body revealed to the doctors that you needed an operation to close the hole in your heart that was pumping blood too strongly into the lungs, making them wet. It would have to be done, they said. The sooner the better. Of course we agreed.

And then, the operation was brought forward because you developed pneumonia. It was brought forward to Thursday,

---

and finally becomes human. There is more than this, for after completing the animal transformation, it passes through the characters in which it appears, in the Negro, Malay, American, and Mongolian nations and finally is Caucasian."

But Dr Down's own son himself pointed out the idiocy of these ideas in 1906: "the characteristics which at first sight strikingly suggest Mongolian features and build are accidental and superficial." For, after all, the Mongolians themselves had 'Mongoloid' children.

August 14th. We were told that there was a risk you might not make it through the operation. It was a serious operation. A certain percentage of children didn't make it. The doctor informed us of these risks with a cassette player recording his words for legal posterity. When I asked about the risks, he dismissed them as being 'only statistical'. What did that mean?

We sat by the bed of this gorgeous girl – yes, you, Stevie – who was sitting up and just getting ready to play in the walking trainer. Your legs weren't quite long enough so you had to tip-toe as you pushed the circular wheeled contraption around the ward. We took it as normal, and it was. But it would never be again.

Bern had misgivings about the day and the date. Thursday is 'day four' of the Chinese week. 'Four' rhymes with 'death'. It was the 14th of the month. I think, at a deeper level, she had true intuitions. Of course I dismissed them out of hand. "Let's just get it over and done with. Then we can get on with our lives." But later I knew she did have intuitions. She had a sense of the impending horror. I came to understand this too late of course.

Thursday came and you went into your operation which required that the doctors knock you out and open your chest, open up the rib cage like a saloon door, and slice through your heart – which of course must be stopped – and fill the hole with cloth, and then sew you back together again. But you may be like the Humpty Dumpty you were beginning to look like. You may not be put-back-togetherable.

There was a three in ten chance you wouldn't make it. Not the tonsillectomy of the cardiac trade that we had at first been jokingly comforted with. And this one-in-700 loser had now become the treasure we stood a close to one third chance of losing.

We closed our eyes and committed your life to the mathematics of fate and wondered how we would look at each other if once again you failed. How precious you were.

And something did go wrong.

Afterwards, you lay on the lambskin rug, a junction of tubes. Your eyes were taped shut. On the blanket, bloodstains. The doctors judiciously reported all the bad news first. The cardiac arrest. The possible failure of the kidneys, the potential brain damage. The inevitability of Hospital Acquired Infection. You lay sedated on your bed – your heart beating with the support of drugs, your lungs ventilated with the support of machines. Your condition was satisfactory, they said.

Your heart had stopped. You were dead. For five minutes your system stopped. A momentary pall on the perfection of things. They came rushing, one assumes, when the heart monitor ceased to plop. They pushed and prodded and squeezed you back to life. Five minutes! And why? No, it didn't stop. That's just what they said at the time. It just slowed down, they said later, so that it was beating terribly slowly, too slowly to pump the oxygen around your brain cells. And why? Because the ventilating tube – which had to be far enough down your throat to ventilate your lungs but not too far down so as to ventilate only one – had been dislodged by a movement of the head. Fate hangs by many a trivial thread. That's what they said at the time – later they suggested that parts of the body had exploded – minute portions of the lung or heart or I know not what had seized up or gone bang, spontaneously, and that this had caused the shutdown in the heart – that was much later when they said this. They said this happened from time to time. No-one knew why. They said it wasn't the ventilating tube. So maybe it wasn't the ventilating tube. Who knows? Fate had it in for you. Who can you blame?

The truth is I could not bear to think of it. I felt so dependent on the goodness and expertise of the doctors. There was a dark abyss threatening to open beneath me, a pit of anger and pain. I closed my mind to it. I didn't want to feel anger. I wanted to feel love. I told myself that there was such a thing as bad luck. You just had to accept it.

A week went by. You lay there sedated – unconscious – for a week. Your body was rigid. Naked. Jammed against the lambskin.

Then, one day, you were awake. You looked beautiful. Your lips were pink, your forehead grew blotchy as you screwed your face up to cry. Dear God!

And then another day and you were out of intensive care. We found you in the public ward. Your eyes stared sightlessly at some constant point in space. Your hands were clenched with remarkable force. What degree of pain and shock were you grappling with? You didn't look at us. Oblivious to our desperate caresses you continued to focus on some bleak inner emptiness. (Oh my dear! My sweet girl!)

And then the doctors began in earnest to talk of 'neurological incompleteness' and temporary, perhaps permanent, damage to nerve centres in the brain. You cried at being touched. You had been assaulted and invaded too much so that each tender caress carried for you the threat of pain. You poor darling! You stared at infinity and clenched the muscles of your legs and arms with impossible force that had nothing to do with desire but automatic compulsion. But still we could not cradle you in our arms as the drip-feed – your lifeline – remained for a week or so plugged into your head. Yes, your head for Chrissakes! We stroked your arms and tried to interest you in music boxes and rattles while the doctors mentioned casually, in parentheses, in a by-the-way mode of speech, that there was always the possibility, which they were looking out for, of spasms or seizures or epileptic fits and if we should notice anything of the sort to let them know.

You went rigid once or twice, your head twisted to one side. Was this it? We mentioned it to the doctors who thanked us for the information but kept their counsel. Gradually you improved. You began to cry in order that we might hold you in our arms. The drip came off. Your heart continued to beat strongly and we were told the operation had been a success. A success? Could they trade off one organ for another and call it success? Perhaps, after all you were alive. Your lungs seemed to be clearing – until you suddenly, inexplicably, began to vomit up viscous custard puddings of phlegm. But your arms and legs had unclenched, more or less. There were the contradictory signs of gradual, uneven, improvements. You were not going to be a vegetable – but would you ever smile again? Would you learn how to walk, swim, run, clamber over rocky shorelines, read, write, talk, laugh, tell jokes, sing and tap dance?

Weeks passed. We kept our eyes open for fits and convulsions but except for this curious way your head would get stuck to one side there was nothing. A neurological paediatrician came and tested you with that indispensable implement, a hammer. A fast stream of inferences drawn and likelihoods expected threw up the words epilepsy and cerebral palsy – and as if hearing this the convulsions revealed themselves the following Monday.

At first only we saw them. Like restlessness or being tossed by ripples from side to side, playfully, momentarily. Between visits, doctors and nurses denied that these had happened but we finally caught one big enough to display with terrible worry for the evaluation of nurses who hummed and huddled before running to telephone the sleeping on-duty doctor who arrived too late to confirm that it was or was not what we all feared.

And of course it was. And when your eyes unglazed and the mind cleared – what could be going on in there? – your eyes glittered and flashed in all directions and we were pleased that you could see again.

Until we were told that you were still blind. At most, all you could see were shadows that obstructed the light. No wonder you didn't smile. And yet...? Could you really not see? You could track a rattle, surely that meant... But no, it appeared it didn't.

"When you talk to her," we were told, "touch her, feel her all over. Rub her with cloths and objects so that she can get the feel of them."

And I felt that I could cope with that until they tested you again and pointed out the clenched fists you maintained and the so-called swordsman posture: your arms and legs tensed and stiffened as your head was moved, forming in repose the classic rapier thrust position and you almost felt you were crying out touché. Classic signs of cerebral palsy. What a dire name. Still another thing. They could turn you into a vegetable yet. Our baby was being murdered. Murdered with names. The person you had been gone. The smile gone. The smile. God damn it, the smile. GONE. The smile murdered. Dead.

And then it was no longer the joy-filled mission to bring up a genetically defective but otherwise full-of-potential complete little being, but the having to deal with a being that had been damaged, knocked about, badly bruised, that had become spastic, epileptic and blind.

What do you do when you can no longer cope? What do you do when you know what you can do when you can no longer cope but you can neither cope nor accept the alternatives?

A question with no answer.

The spasms grew worse. They threw you from side to side with increasing viciousness. Your eyes would go suddenly wide and your head would jerk – this eight month old package of humanity – your mouth would be pulled open as the electric shocks went through you. From side to side. Twisted and thrown. And all I or Bern could do was pat you and touch your face and feel eaten up with guilt at having let the operation go ahead. And hold your tiny hand in ours to give you the comfort that we received from this little act of solidarity – and love and pity and hurt.

Eventually we took you home. The spasms came and went, came and went. You thrashed from side to side ten, twelve, fifteen times a day, for fifteen or twenty minutes at a time – every hour of the day, every two hours at night. From day to day we lived in expectation of new disasters, but there were no new disasters. Just the continuing disaster of your convulsions.

We had a baby bouncer that someone had given us. In the evenings, exhausted, we put you there and watched in shocked despair as you tried to arch your back. The physiotherapist said it wasn't good, we shouldn't encourage it. But it was the only thing that seemed to motivate you. We would rock you a while, then leave you. You learnt to arch your back so that the bouncer bent back and you learnt to kick your legs furiously to achieve this same bouncing motion. For hours at a time you kicked your legs furiously. You got into a lather of sweat but still you wouldn't stop and we were loath to interfere with something that made you want to be. It seemed as if you were addicted but at least you were alive. But the spasms afterwards seemed to be worse. It was a quandary. But we didn't stop it. I think in some way it helped. It was a kind of healing fury.

And still you were grim faced. A baby that doesn't smile? How is that possible? Bern took the hint and held you on her shoulder and bounced you up and down, up and down for up to an hour at a time several times a day, day after day.

Very slowly, infinitely slowly, you improved. First there came the hint of a flexion, a facial twinge, indicating the vague possibility of mirth. But it had to be worked for, and it faded quickly. Bern nearly broke her back bouncing you. The smiles deepened, they reached culmination. They came and went. Oh! You loved to bounce. You loved to be twirled around the room. This was as near to heaven as you could get. You arched your back and bent your head back to get the benefit of the movement. And Bern bounced up and down. You rewarded her efforts with smiles.

Eventually you were not just smiling but laughing. God it was good to hear it. A kind of gulping wheezing sound you made with your mouth wide open and your throat pink. And Bern would dance up and down, up and down until you were laughing and laughing and Bern was laughing too. I didn't have the knack she had. I remember I couldn't keep your neck from flopping forward. I couldn't get the rhythm.

The doctors went from one drug to another in search of that drug that would control the fits and ease the trauma. Gradually, through trial and error, they found a drug that reduced the fits to only six a day.

Getting you to sleep was hard. You would cry for an hour before a sudden jerk would bring it all together. Your eyes, red and bulging, would turn slowly to one side and then the whole body would jerk. Jerk. Jerk. Jerk.

Then you could get to sleep. Only then.

We weren't the only ones with a baby like you.

The idea of forming a group was first suggested to me when you were three or four months old. I had visions of stilted meetings in comfortable middle-class homes. This didn't meet any need I had so we let the idea drift off. It was when you were in hospital having your heart operation that we met a woman who was looking utterly lost. She had a baby with Down's. She also had four or five other children and they lived at the other side of Hong Kong and she and her husband were poor and no-one had told her anything. She was totally bewildered. Her baby was only six weeks old and had a serious heart problem. She didn't know what Down's syndrome was, or what the problem with the heart was or what help there was for her baby, or for herself. No-one had thought to talk to her about the situation. The woman obviously needed help so leaving Bern to talk to her, I went to see the medical social worker who I found with a neat desk and four or five brown folders in front of her.

"I can't just go and talk to her," she said. "She has to be referred. And anyway, can't you see I'm busy?"

I saw in that moment the need for an association that parents could contact and get advice from and where they could meet with others in the same position. Someone suggested that there already was such an organisation so I phoned them.

"I was wondering if you put out information," I said to the person I had been put through to.

"Oh yes. We put out lots of information. To the press. To professionals. To doctors and so on."

"What about to parents?" I asked. There was a long pause.

"Why, that is a good idea!" she said.

I knew at that moment that there was a need for the kind of organisation I had in mind and that I was in a good position to achieve it, being one of that then relatively rare breed, a permanent British resident of Hong Kong. It was my home. I sometimes called myself a white Asian. And Bern was Chinese. We had access to the two communities. We were a good team.

I did not know it then but was to realise later that, almost always, a new idea needs a new organisation to embody it and carry it forward. We needed an organisation that represented the values and interests and concerns of parents. It seemed to me that I was prepared to put three years of my life towards meeting this goal.

And, although it seemed at first, right at the beginning, that my involvement in starting up the organisation was taking me away from you – and Bern and I had a few arguments about whether it was worth it – yes, there were tears and frustrations – I can say that it was a channel for the expression of feelings that could not adequately be expressed any other way.

It took Bern longer to see that the personal pain that is kept inside, dark and secret, hurts for longer. The pain that opens the heart to other people's pain, and leads to helping other people, is a pain that heals itself and enriches awareness. But Bern did in time come to see that, and when she did there was nothing she wouldn't do.

Deciding to start an organisation was the first step, but where were we to go from there? I was introduced to two other parents: Junko Sommerau, the Japanese wife of a Swiss hotel manager, and Kathy Wilman, an Australian. Both had young boys with Down's. Ben, Kathy's son, was as good a role model for the future as any. He had been more or less brought up on a trampoline and was hard fleshed – not loose and flabby as is typical. His pet party trick was to climb up the front of a person and throw himself over the shoulder and climb down the back. He disdained all help.

We became the core. Gradually other parents joined us, some came and went, others stayed. Eventually, we began to gather momentum.

I set it as my ambition to achieve in three years the position where we had an office, a telephone hotline, three staff, a magazine and a million dollars in the bank – (about £80,000 or US$120,000).

It was to take six years.

One mother contacted us. Her story was that when she went to the Government clinic, the doctor, a woman, started making jokes about which of them, the mother or the father, was the idiot because their young baby had a genetic condition, Down's syndrome. She, the mother, had become so depressed because of this she had considered suicide. She only restrained herself because she did not want to cause any more hurt to her husband. We helped her to lodge a complaint. The medical association deliberated and, without questioning the mother, concluded that there was no evidence to support the accusation. Not that they hadn't found any evidence – but that the evidence didn't exist. I have not had much respect for any self-regulating professional body since.

Another mother told us of her husband's experience. While looking at his baby for the first time, he had sensed something was wrong. He had called a doctor who happened to be passing for a comment. The doctor giggled nervously and said: "You're right. He looks like a Mongol."

At one of the early meetings of parents, I found myself talking to the father of a ten year old.

"I don't think I have really accepted my son, even now," he admitted.

Oh yes. There was a great need for an organisation such as the one we were giving birth to.

But the Association nearly foundered before it had got going. The life-or-death debate concerned the name of the Association. I had registered the name as the Down Syndrome Association. I reasoned that as this was the form used in America, Australia and by the WHO, then there was much to be said for it. I was attacked by another active parent who insisted we change it to Down's syndrome as this was the British name and we were living in the then British territory of Hong Kong. I agreed that he had a good case for establishing the name of an association but not a good case for changing the name of one that had already been set up. He said it was grammatically incorrect. I proved to him that both versions were equally correct. It made no difference to him. The things some people choose to consider important, Stevie! Oh Stevie! You would not believe the stupidity of people who are not considered to be obviously handicapped, disabled or impaired.

This argument became heated. I threatened to resign because I was not going to waste three months of paperwork redoing the registration procedures. Eventually this parent backed down. But there was more to come. If I had known of the agonies I would have to go through – the silly, personal antagonisms; the ridiculous manoeuvrings; the petty, furious arguments – I would never have started. Now the Association has over 1,000 members and is very successful – and Stevie, your photograph hangs in the entrance with a plaque that describes you as the Founding Spirit – so I can tell myself it was all worthwhile. It was a good education. But it wasn't easy, Stevie, believe me.

I remember another case that was very instructive. A man contacted me to see if I could help with his brother. The story was this: his younger brother had been born thirty years before with Down syndrome. At that time, the normal, sensible course of action was to put such babies into some form of institutional home and let them (hopefully, one can almost hear the word breathed, albeit guiltily) die of neglect. But in Hong Kong at that time, as with most undeveloped countries, there were no institutions for him to go into. In any case, the man assured me, they wanted to love the baby and do what they could for it, the whole family. I think there had been further tragedy. Perhaps the mother had died. The young boy grew up but was given nothing to do. Loved and cared for in an abstract sort of way, he was nevertheless neglected. Worse: he was adventurous, stubborn, constantly getting in the way, doing things that were unsafe, being troublesome, throwing tantrums when he was obstructed. To deal with the situation they had taken to tying him up. It's possible he was left alone, tied up, in the flat while everyone else went to work and school. I seem to remember the detail that he was put on top of a cupboard.

Certainly, there were reasons that seemed like good reasons for the way things were. But the boy grew. He grew stronger and he grew more frustrated. One day, when he was twelve or thirteen years old, he attacked his older sister. He jumped on her and pinned her down. She screamed and everyone came running. A new element had entered the picture. Now he had to be tied up not for his own protection but for everyone else's. His temper grew worse and his anger and violence grew more threatening. The family could not cope with the situation. They had to move the boy out. But there was nowhere for him to go. Well, not quite nowhere. There was one place. The mental asylum at Castle Peak. In the end that's what they did. They had him placed in the asylum along with the schizophrenics, the paranoid depressives, the violent psychotics and all the others that society felt safer having segregated from normal life. And he stayed there for many years: fed, clothed, washed, given bed space. And possibly it was not the worst place to be. At least he had his freedom, a sort of freedom. And possibly the madness of his new surroundings did not seem to him so very mad. He can't, in any case, have had, previously, a very solid idea of what normality consisted of. He was to be there for many years.

But his brother was disturbed about the situation. He felt there had to be somewhere more appropriate. He approached a woman who was setting up a home for mentally handicapped adults. She told him it would cost him a lot of money, money he couldn't afford. Then he heard of a sort of *ad hoc* centre being run by a priest in Macau. He went to Macau and found that a ramshackle premises was indeed being operated in a loose sort of way as a home for otherwise homeless adults both physically and mentally handicapped. He arranged for his brother to go and live there. His brother was much happier. He was much happier. The reason he was telling me all this was he was wondering if I had any plans to establish an adult residential centre in Hong Kong so that he wouldn't have to travel so far to see his brother.

I was interested in visiting this centre and so, one day, we all went. I had phoned ahead and made arrangements and to get directions. The centre was in a derelict area of run-down factories and squatter huts. The area as a whole had an unsavoury reputation for crime. There were large wire gates at the entrance and behind them stood or sat awkward, angular clumps of humanity. We entered hesitantly. I was carrying you, Stevie, over my shoulder. You were still very young, not too heavy. I guess it was a month or two past your first birthday. I was still new to this game. (Oh Stevie, the adventures you have led me into.) I eyed the men very uncertainly as they moved towards us, gathered near us. Only a few responded to our nods and uncertain smiles. What had we come to?

We found Father Luis Ruiz – short, pugnacious, all heart – in his office. He was happy to show us round. He had done this. He was going to do that. He gestured out his achievements and plans with short powerful arms and the hands of a peasant.

I mentioned that I would like to see the brother. Father Ruiz took me to a room at the back. Here there was a man, shaven, nearly naked, chained to the wall, grunting, sometimes howling, and alternately struggling and shuffling. I stared in horror.

"We have to chain him up. For his own sake." Father Ruiz paused. "But that's not the brother. There's the man you're looking for." He indicated a man who was sitting below a television set. He looked up briefly as I nodded to him then turned away. He was more interested in the comic book in his hands. From time to time he paused to pay attention to the action on television which was showing a costume drama. After a few minutes of that he returned once again to the comic. I had the sense of a man who was quite capable of focusing on the two inputs as and when he chose, without losing his sense of the coherence of either. This was a man who had been described to me as having a mental age of two. He was relaxed and unconcerned about my interest in him though he did look up at me again. I nodded and left him to his twin pursuits.

"I was told he was violent," I said to Fr Ruiz.

"He used to be. But, when I took him to the swimming pool, he didn't know how to swim and he became very angry so I took hold of him and threw him into the water. He immediately calmed down. Water is very calming. He never gets angry now."

Dying from neglect.

There is a condition known as marasmus. It is defined in the dictionary as a 'wasting away of the body'. What the dictionary doesn't say is that, up until the 1920s and 30s, the death rate of children placed in institutional homes was close to 100%. After a year or two of no-one touching them, no-one loving them, no-one showing them the slightest signs of affection, their core of being shrivelled up and dried. They wasted away. They died. They died of the disease called marasmus. Then came a new, bold, innovative approach. It was known as 'mothering'. It involved hugging and laughing and stroking and holding and bouncing and touching – yes, the fundamental, elemental electricity of touch. I think you will agree with me Stevie that we should drink a toast to those men and women who rebelled against the stern, austere coldness of their colleagues, the weight of precedent, and found in their own hearts the answer of love.

Once, at a conference I attended, a professor from Indonesia reported on a ten-year study she had conducted into whether or not there was any advantage in terms of children's development to involve parents in their education. I had to ask myself the question: aren't there some things we can just take on trust? Aren't there some things we can assume? Apparently not. At the same conference, one of the keynote speakers, a representative of an American research institute, reported on a twenty-year study. The objective of the research was to determine whether or not 'early intervention' made any appreciable difference. He did not say how it was that families were directed to his research but those that were, presumably motivated by the promise of regular assessment, were divided into two groups. One group was provided with medical and assessment services alone – but with no educational input. The second group were provided with educational input. When the children in both groups were five years old they were again divided into two groups, with one receiving educational input, while the other group had the educational input discontinued. This meant that there were four groups. One group had no educational input at all, one had input from age five onwards, another up to the age of five but not any more, and lastly there was the group who had received input all the way through. At the age of sixteen, attainment levels were finally assessed.

The results of this research showed, according to the speaker, that at age five there was a significant difference in attainment levels between those receiving educational input and those who weren't. This showed that early intervention up to age five was important. The results thereafter were more mixed; however, it was clear that the group with the lowest attainment levels at the end of the day were those who had not received any input, so the conclusion was that early intervention did achieve results.

But there was something rather unexpected about the results that the speaker avoided mentioning. The group that did best was the group of children who had received early intervention up to the age of five and none thereafter.

"Did you take into account the parents' attitudes?" I asked him later as we milled around the buffet table during the coffee break.

"No," he seemed surprised.

"As I see it, your results argue that the best thing to do is to provide children with early intervention up to the age of five and then to discontinue it."

"Well, yes, I suppose that is one way to interpret the results."

"How would you feel if your child was receiving early intervention and then suddenly at age five it was discontinued? You can see it's making a difference, and you know that other children on the programme are still receiving some form of educational input, and your child is being deprived? What would you do? You would probably do everything you could to educate him the best way you could, either by doing it yourself or putting him in a different programme. And if the researcher asks, just lie and say you're doing nothing so you still get the medical and assessment benefits offered to children who remain in the programme. So, in my view, besides being utterly immoral, your research proves that parents are the most important educational providers there are."

He nodded as though this was a new thought.

"Surely," I continued, "The fact that mentally handicapped children improve when someone teaches them skills is an otherwise not very interesting conclusion. Is it not cruel and unethical to deprive children of intervention that we all in our hearts will be beneficial? Is there not a human right to have such education – and you have deprived these children of their right?"

"You don't know anything about scientific research," he said huffily.

Now, to me, that is intellectual disability.

Do we have to prove that education is beneficial for normal children or can we assume it? Do we have to prove that children do better if someone loves them, and shows they love them, or do we have to prove it?

It would have been nice to have had these thoughts at the time.

As for you, Stevie, the drugs of course worked by making you soporific. With all your learning problems, you didn't need a further damper on your learning abilities. But what could we do?

We had found a balance of two drugs that needed to be carefully monitored because, as you grew bigger, so you would need increasingly more.

And then, slowly, we became aware that the drugs were not quite managing. We were slipping. The spasms were growing more frequent. Everything was beginning, very slowly and frighteningly, to go out of control.

It was then, Stevie, that my decision to set up an Association worked to your advantage. Through this work I had met Brian Stratford, an international authority on Down's syndrome. We got on well and he often came to the island for a drink whenever he was in Hong Kong. He asked me to get your brain scan results to an Italian neurosurgeon he knew, who was 'the best in Europe'. I did as instructed and followed up with details of the doctor in charge of your treatment. Nothing seemed to happen and I forgot all about it. Then, one day, our doctor suggested a new treatment of cortisone injections. She said they would definitely work. By this time my trust in doctors had reached a low ebb and I said I needed to get a second opinion. I went to see the paediatric professor at a leading hospital and he said he couldn't see how the suggested treatment could possibly work. What were we to do? One said it would definitely work, the other said it would definitely not work. I told our doctor of the second opinion. She was not happy. Fortunately, there was a second doctor present, visiting from Glasgow. I don't know what I would have decided if she hadn't been there. However, she offered her opinion that the suggested course of treatment had a ten per cent chance of working. Three opinions: 100%, 0% and 10%. This was certainly evidence that medicine is not an exact science.

In the end, we agreed to go ahead with the suggested treatment which meant that you had to go into hospital for ten days. We were warned that you would feel some discomfort and your temper would not be good. We weren't warned that the treatment was potentially life threatening.

You were placed in a bed immediately below the nurses' observation desk. The idea was that they would keep a register of how many spasms you were having. The next day we asked how many spasms you had had during the night. "None", was the answer. It had worked so quickly? But even as we stood over your cot we could see the waves of a spasm pass over you like soft ripples.

"Look," we told the nurses, "She's having a spasm right now."

"No, she's not."

"She is. That's a spasm."

"No, she's just dreaming."

If only.

There was a girl in a cot near yours. There was something very wrong with her tongue – thick and swollen, it transformed her face, made it seem monstrous. I remember seeing this face and turning away from her in sadness, disgust, pity and horror. She was perhaps two years old. And as I turned away from her, a voice inside me spoke to me, scolded me: She is not a monster, she is a two-year-old girl. She wants love and affection. That's why she's standing in her cot making attempts to communicate. She does not need someone like you to turn away from her in disgust. She needs someone like you to go and be nice to her. To smile at her. To play with her. And the voice was so clearly right that I went over and smiled and touched her and for two or three days we were friends.

And there were other sad children there in that ward. Spastic boys so mangled by the fierce contractions of their muscles. Their mouths dribbled and their yellow misshapen teeth bristled with phlegm. But their dark eyes were saucers of need. They too were just children.

There was a boy, stark and rigid, whose mother had given him a brew of Chinese medicine when only a matter of weeks or months old. It had caused brain damage. How do you forgive yourself something like that?

Dear Stevie, you brought me to dark caverns of need and love and pain.

After a week of treatment they let you out, but for the last three days you had to go back for a daily injection. But the spasms seemed no fewer. So, it hadn't worked. We were so used to failure then, Stevie, that we just gave up. We'd tried. It hadn't worked. Ah well. We were too tired, too dispirited to have any other response. I remember lying with you at night when we wanted you to go to sleep. You cried fitfully through the spasms. Always, before you slept, you had to pass through these spasms, through layer upon layer of pain. Real pain jerked you as you dropped through the layers of consciousness from wakefulness to sleep. I would rhythmically squeeze your foot trying to establish a slow sleepy pulse – and I would think sleepy thoughts so that sometimes it was me who went to sleep first.

It was at this time we had the mad upstairs neighbour. I bawled her out for leaving her dogs to scrape at the floor all night. I, of course, slept like a log, but Bern was disturbed. Perhaps I shouldn't have been so blunt. I should have asked her politely to make other arrangements. She started walking up and down the street at all hours of the night yelling that you were God's punishment on us because we were so evil. After a few weeks of this, Bern threatened to disfigure her. That cooled her down. Then she made a point of making as much noise as possible late at night. I threw a brick through her window. The police came and quieted us down. Such furious fundamental passions.

It became clear that we had to move. The situation was intolerable. But luck favoured us – and our desperation.

Our new flat was the top floor of a two-storey building that looked over a small rocky bay. Fishing junks trawled the shallows near the shore, looming in so near it seemed we could reach out and touch them. In the distance were islands belonging to China.

"And there's China," I said one day to Brian Stratford, showing off my view.

"I always thought China was bigger than that," came the immediate response.

Light flooded into the flat from the vast expanse of sky and sea, a harsh light in the morning sun that turned flat and did strange things to perspective in the afternoon as it veered away behind the house.

At nights, we could sit on our square balcony and watch as fishermen laid small nets by the light of a lamp and then drummed the fish towards it.

So, Stevie, we owe you our home.

One evening, Bern and I were having dinner outside at one of the tables strung along the street outside the restaurant we liked best. It was the time of the Kuan Kung festival. Kuan Kung, General Kuan, is one of the leading Gods of the Chinese folk pantheon. Noted for his red face and proud bearing, he is charged with preserving the moral and political integrity of the Chinese people. On the island, his temple sits inconveniently at the top of a hill so, at the time of his annual birthday, a temporary altar is set up near the waterfront. The altar gave Bern an idea.

"Let's offer a pig to Kuan Kung," she suggested. "Let's pray to him for an end to Stevie's convulsions."

I nodded.

"Well, if we're going to give one to Kuan Kung then we should give one to Pak Tai. He's the main God of the island. If we're going to ask any God we would have to include him," I argued. Bern smiled and agreed.

Of all the Gods, Pak Tai is my own personal favourite. A dark-faced God who presides over the dark end of the year – winter. Under his feet are a snake and a tortoise – creators of havoc. According to local tradition, Pak Tai had, a hundred years before, protected the island from plague. This was a real historical event. Plague swept across south China in the 1870s and 1890s. For a while the people of Cheung Chau were protected by distance and the sea but finally too, plague reached the island. Before the plague arrived, the community of Cheung Chau had been expanding and in doing so they had unearthed a number of nameless, long forgotten graves. It seemed to them the plague was the curse of these uncared-for ghosts.

The people prayed to Pak Tai and a man, who claimed to be in the throes of possession by the God's spirit, insisted on being carried around the island from door to door to bless each household. Soon after, the plague left. Every year the event is commemorated with an annual three-day festival. Tall bamboo towers are erected with strings of white buns tied around them, each bun marked with a livid red stamp. The idea is that all the hungry ghosts – for food is family and hunger is abandonment – are invited to feed themselves. For three days, all the other Gods – represented by their statues – come and pay their homage to Pak Tai. There is much banging of drums and beating of gongs and the rapid drum beat that accompanies the bowing lion dancers. The air is acrid with the smoke of joss sticks. And the highlight is the parade of floats. Each float consists of two young children aged seven or thereabouts enacting some theme or other. Always the girl appears to be standing in mid-air balanced on some improbable support as a cigarette end or a hand-held fan or a tea cup. It is a delightful sight.

We were new to this pig offering business. We ordered two suckling pigs and one or two days later collected them with our barrow. Gleaming mahogany skinned piglets wrapped in translucent red wrapping. We bought joss-sticks, and headed uphill to the temple. As I say, we were new to this business. How long should we leave the pigs on the temple altar? Old men laughed. It didn't matter. And why did we have two pigs? One each for two Gods, we explained. Again they laughed. Wah! One pig is enough. Just take one pig. They won't notice the difference. They laughed to see this lumbering awkward European, this *gwailo*, this 'ghost-man' as they called us in their street slang, with joss-sticks bowing three times to the altar. This *chee-seen*, crazy, *gwailo* who bought two pigs when one was enough!

But we bowed and thought good, clear thoughts for your recovery, Stevie. Please, dear Kuan Kung, please make these seizures go away. Please may the new treatment work. Make it work for our sakes. Please, Pak Tai, Dark Emperor of the North and of Winter, controller of all forces seeking chaos and destruction – symbolised by the cosmic snake and turtle under the soles of your feet – please save Stevie, our daughter, who we love more than anything else in the whole world, who is our life.

If either Pak Tai or Kuan Kung could look into our hearts he would have found no laughter there. We would have done anything, believed in anything. Pascal had a theorem to justify it. If the existence of God is 99.9999% unlikely, one must still believe, for the fruits of belief go only to the believer. And if there is no God, who loses? No one. The end is the same for believer and unbeliever equally.

And then, three weeks later, we suddenly became aware that you weren't having spasms. At night, when you went to sleep, you just dropped straight off. We were able to take you off all medication. We were warned it wouldn't last, that at the age of five, changes in the brain, as it grew and developed, would probably trigger the spasms once again – and they did. But for two to three years it was a sweet relief. God it was good.

I asked Brian Stratford to tell me what he remembered of this time. This was his reply:

> It is remarkable (I refuse to call it merely coincidence) how life presents some kind of pattern. Events are linked in what overall is too well organised to be put down as random chance links arising out of life's 'normal' chaos. My daughter, Philippa, had Down syndrome; she lived for nine years and I felt that her short life had a specific purpose, a destiny which was left to me to fulfil. Stevie had Down syndrome; she lived for almost nine years and had a purpose to fulfil. Her destiny was also put in the hands of her father. Even the differences were part of the purpose, part of the destiny of both our children. Stevie was at the very bottom end of the scale for children with Down syndrome (of which more later), Philippa was at the other end of the scale. This, I believe, was to show us that our measurement of human value is at best pretty crude and cannot be measured in terms of I.Q. Whilst Jonathan had a healthy and well-founded suspicion of 'the professionals' and I was a professional in the field of psychology both of us were basically parents, and like most parents, wanting to do the best we could for our children. Is it any wonder that we were brought together by forces greater than chance ?

I was teaching in Hong Kong, as I did a couple of times a year, preparing Chinese professionally qualified candidates for graduate qualifications at the University of Nottingham. I was also supervising a good number of Chinese post-graduate research students. It was therefore not unusual for umpteen messages to be waiting for me at my hotel when I had been out and for my phone to ring what seemed to be every half hour when I was in. One such message was to the effect that a Chan Berlin, Jonathan, was trying to contact me. No one on my register even approached that name. Ah, a new applicant – No, Mr. Chan, I mentally rehearsed, we are too far into the course to accept new applicants. I resolved to contact him (her?) and suggest waiting six months and enrolling for the next course. But, of course, it was not a prospective candidate, it was Jonathan, who I learned had been trying to contact me at my university department in Nottingham, in the United Kingdom, only to be told that I was in fact in Hong Kong. So that's how I met Jonathan.

I met Stevie for the first time soon after that and my thoughts, after a very cursory examination were, "Oh dear, oh dear, where do I begin?" I am by nature optimistic and I had learned early in my career always to be positive in prognosis whenever this was remotely justified. I looked at Stevie and, apart from seeing a pathetic yet appealing baby, I could see nothing to be positive about. She was obviously profoundly handicapped.

My initial cursory examination told me that if not blind, at best she was only partially sighted; she was hemiplegic, a paralysis of both arm and leg on one side of her body; she was microcephalic, literally a small head, resulting in a much reduced brain weight and compatible with a low level of intelligence. Of course she also had Down syndrome. I remember thinking at the time that the Down syndrome was perhaps the least of her problems, yet she had that inexplicable appeal which is common to children with Down syndrome all over the world. I had said nothing of my deeper concerns to her parents but my first impression was that her life expectation had to be very limited. My impression was founded on a few indicators; her hemiplegia would severely restrict her movement; her impaired eyesight would reduce inquisitiveness and hence her motivation to move; the microcephaly would severely retard her intellectual development. A slight cold, a 'minor' infection, her lungs would fill with fluid and she would fall victim to a pneumonia, the major cause of death in handicapped babies. My second, and lasting, impression was that Down syndrome was perhaps paradoxically her strength. The archetypal personality and general disposition of children with Down syndrome was positively in her favour.

Was I right about her life expectancy? I don't know; at the time I was thinking in months, even in weeks and certainly not years. My daughter Philippa lived for nine years, and as it turned out so did Stevie. Is this limited? How long does a life have to be to be worthwhile or meaningful? Certainly it is short-sighted to confuse time and value as though they are interdependent.

From my professional experience I was pretty sure that Jonathan and Bernie had already been given the kind of pessimistic forecasts that a cautious, generally 'back-covering' paediatrics department would be likely to have given them. I am all too aware of the unspoken but quite clear general message and parents are quick to pick it up: "Please go away and come back when you don't need us." In other words, "We'll make an appointment to see you sometime in the distant future when you have sorted out your own problems, or some other department has become involved. Just don't land on our square." I try to be honest in my professional assessments and clinical judgements, as far as I can be. So ignoring all my misgivings, I said something on the lines of, "Well, let's keep a record of her progress. Let's see how she gets on, how she develops from month to month or even from week to week. I'll ask a current research student of mine to keep in touch and keep the records." I felt so inadequate on the ferry from Cheung Chau to Hong Kong that I could have wept for Stevie, for all children like her and for their parents. I think I did, and fortunately it was late at night, out of season and I was almost alone on the upper deck.

Nothing much happened for a good while. I began to know Jonathan better and we became friends. Not that we didn't have different views or that we always agreed – really firm friends have no need – but I do believe we looked out at the same horizon. Jonathan founded the Hong Kong Down Syndrome Association, an institution which I had been advocating for years but with my sporadic visits to Hong

Kong always tied to University teaching I could never get anything off the ground. And my students seemed to be reluctant to take responsibility for setting up a new venture of this kind. I am proud to belong to that first little group brought together by Jonathan which little by little became the genesis of the Hong Kong association.

During these early years Stevie survived from one crisis to another. I knew that a simple common cold would attack her like pneumonia and measles would be as threatening as smallpox. Sad to say, too often too little attention is given to children like Stevie. They are not so important. "Take your broken doll home" was the 'advice' given to one of my friends in the UK by a woman paediatrician. At best one hears, "Well, it would be a blessing." A blessing to whom?

Some time later, I can't remember when, I was not surprised, but nevertheless shocked (the two can go together) when Jonathan contacted me to tell me that Stevie was sick and deteriorating sharply. She was having convulsions and the frequency was increasing. It seemed that now the 'blessing' was approaching. Jonathan asked me if there was anything I could do. Like him, I didn't believe in these blessings. I immediately phoned Dr. Michael Kidd on the University Medical School line and arranged to meet him in the Staff Club at lunch time. Dr. Kidd is a morphologist and a close friend. He listened to Stevie's history and to her current state. "She needs a really good paediatric neurologist," he said. "There's no one in Hong Kong."

He thought for a while, then said, "There is someone in Beijing, but that would be politically difficult to organise." (This was in former and harder times). "Wait a minute," he said after more thinking. "You will be going to Italy next week and you know Albertini of the Ospedale Bambino Gesu in Rome. He is perhaps the best paediatric neurologist in Europe."

I contacted Albertini, gave him a quick appraisal of her condition and asked him in the meantime, before I went to Rome, to seek the clinical history relating to Stevie from Hong Kong. Dr. Georgio Albertini is a world class paediatrician with a particular interest in neurology and also in Down syndrome. He is also a personal friend (another coincidence?) I accompanied him through his clinics at the Ospedale in Rome, then on to his hospital in Paledora before moving on to his other consultancy at Santa Marinella, seeing countless patients and watching Georgio dictating notes to his tape-recorder or anxious medical secretaries. He does this in a constant stream without apparently breathing. "Has he forgotten about Stevie," I thought, as we drove miles away to the coastal resort of Santa Marinella? No, he hadn't; we were held up at a train crossing (this sort of hold-up goes on for a very long time in that part of Italy) and Georgio stretched to the back of his car for a folder. "The bambina in Hong Kong," he said.

"Yes, I'm worried about her," I said, "Did you receive any information?"

"I receive the case reports from Hong Kong but with great reluctance. They not happy to give information outside their own hospital. I tell them I am Albertini! So they send me case reports after I use strong language in Italian."

"So Georgio, what do we do?"

"The parents, they want this bambina, they want that she live? I think it is they do."

"Yes," I said, "I am sure they want her to live."

"A problem you know," he went on, "She very sick and I ask – do we interfere or do we, well, do we do as Hong Kong do, do we do nothing?"

"So what do you think we should do, Georgio?" I asked.

"I already reply to Hong Kong: cortizona." Albertini gave me the details of the drug, its effect and of the dose he had recommended. "But that is adult treatment," I said. "It will kill her, won't it?"

"She die anyway," replied Georgio as he engaged gear because the train had passed. "This way we might save her. Hong Kong is not too happy you ask me." He laughed.

"It was Kidd at Queen's in Nottingham who reminded me of you. He said that you are the best paediatric neurologist in Europe."

"Dr. Kidd is right," said Albertini. I glanced at his serious face. He wasn't joking.

Well, it worked. Stevie had a good life. It may not have been exciting by 'normal' standards, but she had a good life. She also achieved many things. Without Stevie's existence there would be no Hong Kong Down Syndrome Association, there would be no new and spreading Parents Organisation in the People's Republic of China. I think that Stevie and Philippa have got together about this and they are now somewhere together laughing about the way their fathers are trying as hard as they can to bring about what they intended. Now they know no handicap. Who is going to argue about the quality and value of their lives?

And, yes, Stevie, it worked. For a while. And we were able to relax again, for a while. And we never knew that you were so close to dying. We never knew that every week was a gift of life. And Brian assumes that hints had been dropped. Never. There was never a suggestion. It used to annoy me. I wanted someone to say: Look, this is how it's going to be. But no one ever did. We had to guess. We had to learn day by day how it was going to be. And thinking through what Brian wrote, I think it was best that we didn't know. We might not have fought so hard. We might have hardened our hearts to the future, to protect ourselves.

Instead, we dealt with life as if every judgement was urgent and immediate. Now that the spasms had been brought under control, we started to concern ourselves with your development, to help you acquire skills. What was the point? The point, as I explained to everyone I talked to, was to help you live as happily and to the maximum satisfaction that you were capable. An ambition appropriate for everyone, and certainly not to be denied to you.

And then, sometime around then, your brother Patrick arrived. There had been a miscarriage before that. Bern was always prone to over-doing things, so when she found herself pregnant again we decided to take a break. For years I had been wanting to go down the Yangtze River from Chongqing through the Three Gorges. This seemed to be the right time. We left you in the care of Mary, the first of the maids we had to help us look after you. Focused so closely on our own little world of concerns, we paid little attention to the world at large.

It was early May 1989.

We flew to Chongqing where we boarded the ferry that was to take us down the first stretch. Halfway through the Gorges there was a side trip to what was known as the Little Gorges. Here a stream of crystal clear waters plunged down into the thick sludge brown of the Yangtze. Powerfully built peasants hauled the boats up the rapids. This was another world, one which, apart from the souvenir shops at the village which acts as terminus for the day trip, would have changed little in two thousand years. An idyll. A momentary reprieve from the modern world.

The return was even more dramatic as we skipped and skated down the even white spume and froth of the river – so smooth and white it looked like one could jump out and slide down – as indeed you probably could.

Another ferry took us through the remaining Gorges. The water was low and vicious reefs of rock were exposed. The cliff faces stretched high above us, made of crumbly, rotten limestone much of the way. At every town and every bend numbers were etched into the rock face. Flood tide marks stretched up to as high as sixty metres. The towns along the way were grimy, ugly places. There were perhaps three buildings along the way that one would regret the destruction of. But the Little Gorges. I will miss them.

At I-Chang, the other end of the Gorges, we got off the ferry and took the train to Wuhan, a city formed by the junction of three cities, one of which was Hankow, from where China clippers raced each other to London with their cargoes of tea. When we got off the train there was a small demonstration of perhaps fifty people marching and chanting. They were carefully policed but there was no sense of crisis or urgency or violent passions. The ticket collector of the minibus we were on waved a cheerful, supporting, thumbs-up sign.

We found an old, crumbling hotel in what had been the European quarter that smelled of better times long gone. Here, as we strolled in the evenings, we became aware of muted gatherings in the dark. People came together for quiet discussions in small groups which then quickly broke up only to reform elsewhere.

After a day in Hankow we decided to go to Beijing.

"Not possible," said the clerk at the travel desk.

"Why not?"

"The situation," was all he would say. In our naïvety we thought he meant the transport situation. We still didn't feel like returning to Hong Kong so we boarded another ferry and sailed down to Shanghai. It was an uneventful journey, the value of which was that Bern was not able to over-exert herself and so Patrick survived that dangerous period between the second and third month.

In Shanghai we made straight for the Peace Hotel and were given a room overlooking the street. The beds, along with the rest of the furniture, came straight from the thirties. The springs squeaked and squawked at every movement but the bedrooms equipped with modern beds faced on to a dark interior well so we decided to put up with the complaining springs.

It was only now that we realised how precarious the situation was. On the way to the room I picked a free copy of the *China Daily* from the newspaper rack. The front page screamed urgent headlines. I learnt that the people of Beijing had put barricades across the streets in the suburbs to keep the army out. Oops! Below us in the street serious demonstrations were taking place. "Down with Li Peng! Down with Li Peng!"

The first plane we could get on was in ten days' time. Ten days! Everything was booked up until then. So we had time to explore Shanghai and the canals and gardens and pagodas of Suzhou. Every day we checked the newspapers. Everything seemed calm, controlled. It would work out. We weren't really worried. On Sunday June 1st, we took a taxi to the airport. On the way we saw children all dressed up carrying toys and balloons.

"Must be a birthday party," I commented to the taxi driver who was practising his English on us.

"No. Today is International Children's Day." He seemed surprised I wasn't aware of this.

Three days later the tanks rolled into Tiananmen Square.

Bern insisted on having an amniocentesis test. I was against the idea but she closed her mind to any discussion. It's true the risk of miscarriage was slight – but there was a risk – variously estimated as somewhere below 1-2%. How silly to undergo even such a low risk. But Bern was adamant. And what were we going to do if a problem was found?

"Whatever she wants to do," a friend advised.

"But what about me? Don't I have a say?"

But there is no possible answer to the conundrum. There is no possibility of a negotiated compromise. It would have to be one way or the other. Someone had to make that decision. But I wasn't happy.

We went together to the hospital to be counselled. We were shown a video. It showed two adults with Down Syndrome. This was the reason we were having the amniocentesis – so that we wouldn't have another child like you, Stevie. I couldn't accept that. But I decided to bide my time until there was something to discuss. I was appalled at the size of the needle that they plunged into Bern's taut swollen belly as they used an ultra-sound machine to see where the baby was. They didn't want to plunge the needle into a head! And the result was clear. Our baby was normal. And there was no miscarriage. And Bern felt much happier. And I was left with my nagging concern like a dull toothache.

Six months later, Patrick was born. The waters broke at about eight o'clock in the evening. We went to the local island hospital. A police launch took us to Hong Kong where an ambulance was waiting to take us to a hospital. They insisted they had to take us to the Government hospital. We had already made arrangements to be admitted to another hospital so when we arrived, we discharged ourselves and caught a taxi. It wasn't far. Midwives whisked Bern away and I left Bern, not realising things would happen so quickly. When I returned early the next morning Patrick was already born.

"How was it?" I asked the midwife.

"Bad," she said.

"How do you mean?"

"The baby was blue."

Oh Stevie! I was so scared.

I went upstairs to check on Bern. She caught my arm. "There's a little problem," she said.

Did she know already?

"What problem?"

"It's a boy, not a girl." We'd been told, after a scan, to expect a girl. She smiled tiredly.

"I think we can manage with that," I assured her. I didn't tell her what the midwife had said.

The next two hours were bad. Was it possible to have two damaged babies? I prepared myself for the worst news. When at last I got to see the doctor he did not seem too bothered. Yes, the baby had been a bit blue.

"What about brain damage?"

"Oh no. He's fine."

And indeed he was, and is, and, touch wood, will be for a very long time.

I was giving a talk to some occupational therapy students and I was stressing the point that the only way we could maintain our sanity was for us to recognise that everyone in the family had needs

– and no-one's needs should be neglected. Also that we needed to maintain a sense of balance within the family.

"But how is that possible?" asked one of the students. "When you have to spend so much time looking after such a handicapped child, you have to do everything for her. How can you retain a sense of balance?" It was a good question. And the answer, Stevie, as you know, over the years, you had your special friends who helped us look after you.

First there was Mary. She was a strong but unhappy woman who left vapour trails of depression throughout the flat. Her husband was seeing another woman. That was why she had decided to come to Hong Kong, leaving behind a small business in the Philippines. It was an unsatisfactory arrangement in many ways. Mary had no particular wish to be a domestic helper. Her one objective was to keep an eye on her husband. She grew to love you Stevie, as we all loved you. But she was moody and her moods affected the way we all felt.

After a year or so, to our relief, she decided to leave us and that's when Daisy came to join us. Daisy was easier, a lighter presence. Always willing. Daisy was a good friend to you, Stevie. But after two years, Daisy too left us to get married and have children of her own.

That's when Del came. Del was a strong character and also subject to moods. We started to go through a larger number of glasses than normal. The sound of breaking glass from the kitchen became a regular accompaniment to our life. But we never said anything. What were a few glasses if they were the price of peace? And with you, Stevie, she was good. She loved you and wanted you to develop in any way that you could.

But as you grew it became clear that we had to employ a second helper. You were getting heavy, Stevie, and you needed to do exercises – and we wanted someone to cover every Sunday and other holiday for the simple reason that we were exhausted. So we asked Del if she knew someone she could work with and share a room with and she suggested her niece Lyn. So Lyn came to join us. Lyn seemed to float airily around the flat. There was no sense of compulsion or decision but the things that needed to get done got done, and got done effortlessly. Lyn brought a great quality of ease and peace with her.

How strange it was for us to have these foreign presences occupying our small flat. We were unused to having someone else so permanently there. It was not a big flat. It was a constraint. I think this played a part in the slowly widening chasm that opened up between us, your Mum and me. We could not relax in quite the same way as we could before – no silly, sudden sex; no long, languorous huggings and kissings. There was always someone there. Always a constraining witness. But what was the alternative? And anyway, isn't it true that this is the fate of all married couples: the children do get in the way, especially if, as is the Chinese way, they stay in the bedroom until they are three or four or even five or six years old.

How could we have coped without Mary, Daisy, Del and Lyn? The simple answer is that we couldn't have. But in Hong Kong domestic help was cheap. Two maids cost perhaps a quarter of my teacher's salary. We were very lucky to have a country as impoverished as the Philippines in the neighbourhood.

The only alternative would have been some form of hospital care. I once visited the ward of a hospital where severely and profoundly handicapped children – some abandoned, others visited, regularly or irregularly, by family members – were cared for. The sheets were immaculately starched. The walls were white. The nurses and doctors were dressed in white. The old building gleamed piously and sinlessly white – the whiteness of witless care. Where were the slashes of colour to awaken the soul? The ward creaked with hushed goodness. Where were the sounds for joy to dance to? Only the crackle and static from a cheap television. Spastic arms had been deliberately trapped under table tops to stop them waving them about with spastic exhilaration at the joy of movement. Every child had a tube in its nose. For food. No possibility of succulent masticatory pleasures. Many children lay prone or supine in toyless, colourless cots. One nurse for twenty-five beds. No time for the sensory tactile pleasures of touch. The coma of waking consciouslessness. The sheets stainlessly crisp and white. No, Stevie. We could not ever have considered that. Please God no. We were spared that agony.

Once, in a south-east Asian country that I prefer not to name – because it is, of that I am certain, no different from other developing countries – I was attending a conference on mental retardation. We were taken to visit a Government centre that was underfunded. Of the six hundred children at the centre, a decent level of care could be provided to about two hundred. I was not fully aware of the situation as I strolled about the facility, admiring small workrooms and performances. Suddenly I became aware of an odour that I had smelled before. It was the hot, fetid, heavy scent of piss and shit. It took me back to the Cat House at London Zoo as it was in the mid to late fifties. I had been taken there at the age of five or six and again when I was ten. I remember the tigers, lions, leopards, panthers pacing backwards and forwards, grimacing, whiskered snarls as they paced back and forth, back and forth. And the smell of the cat shit! Overpowering. But this was no zoo. Where did the smell come from? There was a concrete block not far away with a wide flight of stairs. I walked hesitantly up to the next floor. A door opened on to a room the size of the entire block – an empty concrete room devoid of furniture. Inside were some fifty or so naked children. Children who it was clear did not have clothes, never wore clothes. Most sat staring blankly, without any form of expression, large headed, gaunt. Empty souls. Nameless. Not even numbered. Utterly without identity. The floor was a cesspool. It was being hosed down. The children were being hosed down. That was it. They were fed, they were hosed down. That was it. That was their life. Their short life until they caught pneumonia and died. All this was evident immediately, at a glance. And when I had finally understood what it was I was seeing I felt sick and I felt culpable.

Belsen? Auschwitz? Buchenwald? No, I am being excessive. Surely?

Back at the workshops, one of the lucky ones, a seventeen year old, was showing us around. It was clear that he belonged here but the strange thing was that he could speak reasonable English. And he seemed bright. How could such a child be placed in an institution like this? Surely he wasn't handicapped. I asked what the criteria were for admission. If the child could not speak at the age of six they were considered to be handicapped, I was told.

I mentioned to the Australian girl sitting next to me on the bus taking us back to our air-conditioned luxury hotel that I, who did not start talking till the age of four, and Einstein, who had not said anything till he was five, were lucky.

"My grandmother didn't speak until she was eight," the girl told me. "She went on to become the first female president of the Australian Psychological Association."

I sometimes think about that boy.

Ah Stevie, I remember your wonderful lustrous eyes that flashed from side to side as you listened to music, or when someone made a muted chant of your name: Steeevie! Stevieeee! Steeeeevieeee!! Your eyes would open wide with pleasure and your mouth too would open in ecstatic pleasure.

But it was your ears that you used to mediate your inner world and the outer world of us and the doctors and the noises of every day around you.

I often used to ponder this question: what thoughts did you have? What mental images registered on the screen of your mind? What understandings did you have? Did you recognise any of us? Did you know I was your Dad? Did you have any understanding of what Dadness might be?

Once or twice you were asked to attend special training sessions. There you would be used to assess the diagnostic abilities of trainee doctors. Down syndrome, they got easily, then, when prompted, your spasticity, but the fact that you were blind, this was very far from being apparent to them. A psychologist friend insisted you could see. He insisted that your eyes and his met when he came into the room where you sat supported by cushions, a reclining princess, listening to your tapes of music. Not staring intently but momentarily stopping and for a brief second a kind of click of visual connection before flashing elsewhere in response to some internal imperative. Louise too commented on it. A friend and neighbour, she had taken to visiting you and sitting with you. She too insisted that you could see. A visiting Australian specialist was of the same opinion. He pulled a striped tie across the path of your vision and your eyes caught the pattern and checked and followed, briefly, for a thoughtful moment. Certainly there was nothing wrong with your eyes. It was just that the parts of the brain whose job it was to decode these messages didn't work. Or did they? Or was it just light and dark and two dimensional shapes, but not shape or distance or relationship. The deconstructions of a single, seemingly simple, skill.

But you never were to use your eyes to take in messages, to feed the mind with information, to make contact with us who were out there beyond the confines of your transient impulses. Perhaps also it was because you had focused your attention on hearing. You could hear so well.

I can see you still reclining, your mouth is open with a kind of intense concentration on the music. From time to time your mouth widens, a kind of gasp as whatever it was hit some spot of pure pleasure. Your right arm would rise slightly in the air. Sometimes, when the pleasure was intense you would hold out both arms stiffly and try to kick. Oh those songs that you listened to day after day, those songs that were your whole world of pleasure and meaning. You never tired of them. Year in, year out, you listened to the same songs. What would we have done without them? What would your life have been like?

One of the little mysteries we discovered was just how good the local Chinese tapes were. They collected all the standard children's songs and strung them together, never allowing one to end abruptly. A woman's voice linked one to another. The English and American tapes however were just so many tracks of sub-operatic warblings coldly rendered. They started and ended abruptly. There was no understanding that they would be listened to by children. And for blind children – for you Stevie, and children like you – the sudden abrupt starts and finishes left your nerves jangled. You always cried. You had three favourites tapes that we played and played again. You were washed in this sound.

When a tape finished you would start to cry – not tears, not pain but a signal for attention: eh! eh! eh! pause. Was anyone coming? Eh! eh! eh! "What's wrong Stevie?" we would say as we came running in. As if you could tell us. But it was always the music. The tape needed to be turned round. Often we would go into your room, beckoned by your cry. "What's wrong Stevie? What's wrong?" Strange. The music was still on. What could it be? And then the music would suddenly snap off at the end of the tape. You could predict when the tape was going to end! This was even more impressive than appears at first sight because different tapes had the same songs in varying orders. In any case, what did you know of machines, and sides, and cassettes that needed turning over. All you knew was the songs had an order and if you said 'Ugh! Ugh!' somehow they would start again. What cleverness was trapped inside you? What intelligence were you capable of that we could never reach? What potential would never be realised?

This was a question that I asked myself many times over the years. It was a question that could never be answered.

> Twinkle twinkle little star
> How I wonder what you are
> Up above the world so high
> Dah de dah de dah de dah
> Twinkle twinkle little star
> How I wonder WHO you are

One day, as I was humming this song to myself, which I did with curious frequency, I was reminded of a snatch of poetry.

> But you are greater than the world
> Though you are such a dot
> For you can think and feel
> And the world cannot.

Where did that come from? And was it true? Let a hundred philosophies contend. I didn't care. It suited my sentimental mood.

At the age of three, you needed to proceed to some form of school. The only school that seemed to be doing anything interesting was run by the Spastics Association. It was a modified form of a Hungarian system known as Conductive Education. The principles were that children had to use furniture that was solidly made and shaped precisely to their scale. Handicapped children had to learn to achieve goals through their own conscious effort and through intensive exercises. For Hong Kong this had been watered down. We decided to enrol you on this programme and you were accepted.

Stevie, I'm so sorry. Wisdom always comes late, after the event. We did not learn until much later that specialists in Conductive Education specifically exclude the blind from their programmes. And so we entered a period of nearly two years where you would stay as a weekly boarder at a small centre. You slept there for four nights a week and came home for three.

A typical day went like this: You would be lifted out of bed into a chair and strapped in. Your legs were strapped so that the knees were both bent – your arms were strapped firmly at the elbows to keep them straight and you were given a rail to hold. You had your own free-standing stand which consisted of horizontal metal tubes fixed to two vertical wooden supports. This was one of the central fixtures of your treatment. When you ate, your hands were placed round the metal tubes; and also when you squatted over the potty for your regulation, ritualised potty session – eight nappies a day you went through, most of them clean. When you did your walking session this stand was there for you to lean against. Walking required two people to help: one behind holding the hips and pushing the legs. The one in front holding the arms. These helpers sat on low, wheeled, cushioned stools. I can still remember the feel of the rhythm of this walking exercise, the cajoling words, the shift of weight, the pressure on our own arms. But it was good exercise – for all of us.

Then there were the benches with slats for gripping as, in theory, you learnt to pull yourself forward but instead slid as we pushed you along the smooth, polished surface of the wood.

The feeding was the most difficult. You sat at a specially made chair with a table on which there was a metal rod for you to grasp hold of. From behind you, with my left hand I held your head up by cupping you under your chin while I spooned in the green and white sludge that you would let dribble out. Even with tasty mushy sweetened apples you would pull your funny quizzical expression. You needed the food to be carefully spooned in. This was tiring and it fell to me to do when you were home. And, when I was used to it, it became a kind of meditation.

But it was the nights, four nights alone all night surrounded by other crying babies that you couldn't see. Four nights of crying yourself and not hearing the friendly, known, soothing voices – only the voices of strangers. Four nights of no music. A small little hell. I'm so sorry, Stevie. Perhaps we needed the space, the time of not having to care for you every second of the day. Perhaps that's why we allowed ourselves to ignore how unhappy you must have been in this school four nights a week. Oh and the delight on your face when, on the Friday afternoon we brought you home, and set you up against the cushions and switched on the cassette player.

> Twinkle twinkle little star
> How I wonder what you are.
> Up above the world so high,
> Like a diamond in the sky...

This was your favourite song. We could always get a smile out of you by singing it.

And then you started running fevers. The only way you could express your unhappiness. We would be phoned to come and take you away at all times of the day. And you weren't improving. You weren't able to do anything new. For a while we tried to guess that we saw signs that you were improving somehow or other. But of course you weren't. You were just fed up and puzzled and lonely. But what was the alternative?

Finally we realised it didn't make sense. We would have to keep you at home and hire a second domestic helper to help take care of you. So we brought you home.

At about this time I came across references to the Doman-Delacato method. They were all highly critical and warned parents not to believe this charlatan. But some articles, by parents, said that they had very successfully followed this kind of therapy. What kind of therapy? The articles were not very clear. I discovered that Doman was an American physiotherapist who believed that intensive physical activities, the movement of limbs in set sequences, tailored to each child's particular problems could, in a number of cases, lead to drastic improvement in developmental terms.

I discovered there was a centre in Devon that taught a modified version of his system. Instead of doing the exercises 12 hours a day, they only needed, they said, to be done three hours a day. Only.

My father knew of a girl who had benefited from a programme of activities developed at this centre. A girl who had only been able to stagger from place to place could now run more or less normally.

One of the problems of these programmes was that they required a great deal of community involvement. Often an activity might require four people. There had to be a string of volunteers. And the emotional strain on the family, we were warned, was great. We decided to investigate this option. But first we had to get back to Britain.

I remember that flight very clearly. Patrick was nine months old and so we reserved a bassinet and two front row centre section seats. We booked two seats in the row behind for you and Daisy, who was accompanying us. We were a little worried about how you would cope on the flight. You did not have the muscular control to sit and there wasn't room in a seat for you to lie down. And of course you had to have your music. Fortunately the plane was not completely full and the air stewardess shuffled passengers around. Stevie, you were able to lie across three seats with ear-phones on. But it must have seemed so strange to you: all these new noises. What sense could you make of them?

And Patrick too had a wonderful flight. It was a fourteen-hour, one-stop flight. And Patrick didn't utter a sound. He sat in his bassinet and just watched wide-eyed at all the people who passed by. In the next bassinet, the occupant was less happy and cried more or less continuously but Patrick paid no attention. A stewardess whisked him off for a little trip to the galley and ten minutes later he came back as unworried as he had been before. During the second leg of the trip, he came to the notice of a group of some fifteen to twenty French tourists who occupied a block of the side seats. They started waving and cooing and continued to wave and coo for the rest of the trip. They became utterly infatuated with him. I even saw a man several rows back elbowing his companion to get him to get Patrick to look in his direction. It was infatuation pure and simple. And dear Patrick sat blissfully unconcerned the whole trip. I don't think he made a single sound the whole time. He just sat up and watched contentedly as the world went by.

Back in England, we drove down to the centre and spent two days there. You were assessed and a sequenced programme of exercises was prescribed, and we were taught how to carry them out. There were the arm and leg exercises where we had to move your arms and legs together in certain simple combinations. We had to roll you over. Bend your legs up together and back again. Then we tried to force you to crawl across the floor by moving your arms and legs appropriately and letting you get a sense of movement. We also had to hang you upside down. You complained violently about the crawling. You cried. It was uncomfortable. But being upside down did not cause you any problems. At most you had a vaguely quizzical expression on your face. 'What are they doing to me now?' you seemed to be saying, using your own interior means for talking to yourself.

The director of the centre told us it was his belief that the cerebral cortex – the layer of brain that wrapped the rest of the brain like a kind of parcel wrapping – could relearn skills normally controlled by other parts of the brain which had been injured. He admitted this was radical and not widely accepted. As I subsequently discovered, most doctors said it was complete nonsense.

And did the exercises do any good? Not in the sense that you showed any measurable improvement. But they gave us a focus, and gave you some exercise. They were a way of marking the day. We mixed the exercises you had done at the conductive education centre with the new ones we had learnt. We invented our own, manageable, programme. It kept us all sane.

But gradually it became clear that you weren't going to improve. That you were going to remain very much as you were for the rest of your life, however long that might be. And when we came to that realisation we started to relax. It took a lot of pressure off us.

The way I put it to myself was this: you had been very unlucky. Unlucky didn't seem to do justice to what you had been through. But you were happy listening to your tapes. You were kept fairly healthy with the exercises. And our job was to keep you feeling happy. What life you had should be satisfying. And happy you were, amazingly enough, until the end.

Health was a problem. You spent most of the time lying propped up against cushions. You weren't exercising your lungs. No-one had warned us this was going to be a problem. You, in any case, having Down syndrome, had low immunity to colds and so on. It grew on us slowly that this was going to be the big problem.

One day, I read in the newspaper – or was it a television programme I saw? (I can see it so clearly) – a story about a woman who had adopted a child who had been born essentially without any brain – the centre of his brain was missing. All he had was the cerebral cortex. But he hadn't died as he had been expected to do and at the time of the story was eight or ten. His adoptive mother said they often watched television together and the boy would laugh, even though he was blind. He spent hours watching television and laughing. As I took in this story I felt a little ill. Maybe all the behaviours you had that I associated with intentional, mentally significant activity were nothing more than brainless, automatic responses. Or did this boy not have intelligent existence, as the mother clearly believed? Could the cortex take on mental functions as some believed?

What is intelligence? At base, is it not simply the light of conscious awareness? Certainly, damaged as you were, Stevie, you were human. Your understanding of the world was that of a human – an intelligent human being – whose potential for understanding the world had been damaged: your ability to take in the data of the world had been damaged and your ability to process and make sense of the data had been damaged. But the baseline of your existence was your humanity and your intelligence.

What then is it that is being measured by IQ tests? The degree of awareness? To a limited extent. These tests generally test abilities. Often, they test the speed at which these abilities can be brought to bear successfully on a problem. The problems generally require various forms of analytical reasoning and brain-body (known generally as hand-eye) co-ordination. Of course there must be different tests for different age-related cohorts of test takers as people at different developmental stages have different consciousnesses. Ideally, the tests have been standardised over large populations of people of various ages so that an average score for any age band can be established. Once the bell curve of scores for each age group has been established, the peak point of the curve becomes the measure of average mental age for that age group. So the equation for intelligence is mental age divided by chronological age multiplied by 100. An IQ of 100 represents absolute average normality. If your level of intelligence falls in the range 70-130 you are of normal intelligence. If your IQ is 69 you are below normal, if your IQ is 131, you are of above normal intelligence. It's that simple.

There are many disagreements about what it is that standard IQ tests are measuring and some psychologists have proposed that there are as many as eighteen different forms of intelligence, many of which are unmeasured by standard tests: musical intelligence, athletic intelligence, strategic intelligence, visual intelligence and so on.

And what about you Stevie? Of course all of this is meaningless as far as you are concerned. Well, not quite meaningless. I was talking one day to the director of a centre for blind students. They had a section for the mentally handicapped. At that time we were swimming in the heavy waters of life trying to make decisions without fully understanding the situation.

"I need your advice," I told him. "You see, we've been told that Stevie is blind but we want to do something for her. We want to reach her. She's intelligent. We know that."

"Well," the director paused. "For children who are only mildly handicapped..."

I realised immediately the misunderstanding that had occurred.

"No, sorry. I must clarify the situation. Stevie is severely and profoundly handicapped. She can do nothing for herself. She can't sit up, roll over, speak or even suck her thumb by herself. But there is this light in her eyes. There is this way of sensing she has. She questions things. She has this intelligence. I have no other word for it. She has intelligence. We can't measure it, but it's there. Her eyes are luminous with her mental being." Yes, of course I didn't say all that to him, but I would have if I'd had the words for that was the truth of it.

There were times when I would silently open the door to your room. You would be listening to the cassette. I would push the door open and step in as quietly as I could. Your hands would be working up and down and your feet with the fun of it. Your mouth wide open and laughing. Your eyes glinting in pure pleasure. Then after a few moments your eyes would start to stray towards the door. You knew something was there. What? What was it? But you knew no threat. You had no fear. All presences were friends. But you knew some living being was there. Yes, Stevie. You had your understandings. You had your thoughts. But what they were, what shape, form, texture or colour they had, we will never know.

It was a Sunday, early afternoon. You were lying on your bed wheezing. You'd had a cold for a few days. I was feeling low for some reason. I was having a beer. And then Daisy, your special friend, called me urgently.

"Sir! Come!"

I sauntered into your room. You weren't looking too well. Then all of a sudden you stopped moving. You stopped breathing. You no longer had the effort to breathe in and out. Slowly you turned blue. Oh Stevie. I was tired. A very cold voice inside me said maybe this is for the best, let her go. For a long cold moment I wanted it all to be over. But Daisy started to keen, not cry or sob but keen. She knew what was happening. Maybe she knew what I was intending. And the high sharp note of her crying brought me suddenly to a full realisation of what was happening and I picked you up and started to run to the hospital barefoot down the concrete path. And that's what saved you. If we had been living in an apartment block with a lift you would have died. But as I ran you slapped into my chest. All I could think of was don't step on a nail or a brick or a stone. I kept my eyes on the path, running as fast as I could and I had run perhaps two hundred yards before I thought to look at you and your cheeks were pink and I knew then you were OK.

At the hospital they told me you had pneumonia and they called for a helicopter. In fifteen minutes we were down by the helicopter pad and you were loaded on board. I climbed in with you. Then we were off across the channel of ship-studded water, around the bend of Hong Kong Island, across the harbour and down to the landing pad by the Queen Elizabeth Hospital on Kowloon peninsula. There an ambulance took us across the road to the emergency room. Suddenly you were taken away from me. A flurry of green cloaks surrounded you. A curtain was drawn. I was asked to sit down and wait. What was happening to you? I felt it was wrong that I should so suddenly be excluded. Then the crisis was over, it seemed, your condition was diagnosed and dealt with. You were admitted to a ward. We didn't know then that you would be in there for three months and in the end we saved your life by taking you away.

First there was the pneumonia, then when that seemed to go there was hospital acquired infection. There was a constant battle with bacteria. Weeks became months. No one told us what was happening to you. I remember being at your bedside one day watching the doctors huddling with their files and reports. I was waiting for an opportunity to catch one and ask for an update. I became aware that they were aware that I was waiting. Finally a young woman doctor stomped across the room to me.

"What do you want to know?" she demanded angrily. I was surprised but had the wits to say: "What should I know?"

She gave me an answer at a hundred miles an hour.

Then one day we became aware that you were starting to grow fatter. It was happening at an alarming rate. Day by day you were visibly blowing up like a balloon.

"What's happening?" we asked the doctors.

"We're giving her a lot of milk protein."

"Does she need so much?"

"Yes. It's not too much."

"Look at her. She's getting very fat."

"We can't do anything about that."

"Well, why does she need so much?"

"She has blood sugar problems."

That's how they told us you had blood sugar problems. Bern started to panic.

"We must get her out of here."

"We want to move her to another hospital," I told the doctor.

"Impossible. She can't be moved. She's our patient."

"Your patient?" I had a sudden thought. "Actually, she isn't your patient. She's really a patient at Queen Mary Hospital on Hong Kong side. That's where all her records are. That's where we've always taken her before. Or to the Duchess of Kent Hospital for children. She's only here because of an emergency."

The doctor wanted me off his back.

"I'll see what I can arrange."

Two days later you were transferred to the Duchess of Kent Hospital. The presiding doctor took one look at you and refused to accept you. So up the hill you went to the Queen Mary Hospital where the doctor in charge thought you were at death's door.

"How far do you want us to go to keep her alive?" he asked.

"As far as with any other child," we told him, "but no life support system."

The next day you were over the worst and the day after I talked to the doctor. He was a complete change from what we had been used to. He was approachable, clear, concerned.

"Are you going to put her back on the ten pints of milk a day that she's been on?" we asked.

"Ten pints?"

He looked at us as if we were mad.

"For the blood sugar problem."

"What blood sugar problem?"

"The blood sugar problem that the doctors at Queen Elizabeth Hospital said she had and that's why they were giving her ten pints of milk a day because of the protein..."

I really didn't understand what I was saying.

"She doesn't have a blood sugar problem," he assured us.

"Oh!"

So what would have happened to you if we'd left you where you were? And how could a whole team of doctors come to the wrong conclusion about you? But we didn't pursue it. We had become used to feeling like victims of the medical process. We behaved like victims. The less we had to do with it all the better.

And so, over the next few weeks you deflated until you were almost back to your old self. It was a new building, a clean building, and so your hospital acquired infection quickly cleared up and you came home to us again.

I think it was now that we realised that one day you were going to die of pneumonia. We didn't know when but that's how it would be. And until then we had you and your smile, your happiness, your love, your little joys. But we didn't know it strongly. It was just the shadow of knowledge. And we saw clearly that you weren't going to develop any further. You weren't going to sit up, or roll over, or feed yourself, or kiss...

Kissing you. Of course, we loved to sit with you and hug you and kiss your soft smooth terribly white skin. But if we kissed you on the lips or put our cheeks next to your lips you responded with an expression of the most fastidious distaste mixed with wondering. What was this sensation? What did it mean?

Now I can sit back and write it down and come to some approximate interpretation of events but then we were too close, too defeated, too exhausted. Perhaps we should have given you a curriculum of tactile sensations. But what, after all, would you have done with them? You cringed away from the cool breezes of the outdoor world. You had no control over them. They disturbed your sense of identity, unity. And they were beyond your control. Perhaps over and above the joy you got from the music – an unchanging joy which never dissipated into habituated boredom – each song was fresh, known and welcomed with the joy of recognition – was the fact that they helped to order the blackness of space, to give dimension to the geometry of time. I can only spin words to create unlikely nuances in the hope that the poetry of thought can create some conception of how life might seem to you if you were only conscious enough to see yourself for a moment as we see you. But I am left with the vast mystery of how the world may have seemed to you. When you woke, were you then aware of waking and sleeping as being distinct and of now not sleeping? Was waking any different from sleeping? Did the dreams of waking life differ from the dreams of the night-time? Could you see light and dark, shape and colour – not dimension or perspective, we knew that, but something... please God something.

And we did massage you. Every part of your body was smoothed by strong hands so that you could have a tactile sense of your dimensions, of your shape, of the parts that made up your body: arms, legs, back, buttocks, neck, fingers and toes, nose and ears, all your extremities, so that you could have some understanding of the sensual possibilities of your own body, for how else would you know?

Our flat overlooked the rocks of a small bay. There were sea sounds. How did they seem to you: these sounds of water lapping against the sand, the slow suck of the tides, the crash of waves, the beating of wind and rain against the windows, the whistle of wind, the rustle of leaves in the trees outside? Sometimes, you would cock your head wonderingly at these new sounds, that strange, funny way you had of withdrawing your lips, mouthing an Oh.

Sometimes I would come into your room quietly and stand there. We could see the showers stream in towards us from the sea – but you were locked into your songs and we shrugged our shoulders. What could we do? Was it not enough simply to enjoy the life we were given? We could not make you better, or different. But we could make what life you had comfortable. It was all we could do. I'm so sorry Stevie that we couldn't do more.

But you can't stop growing. I liked to lie on my back with you on my belly on the brackets of your arms and elbows. "Come on Stevie. Lift your head. Lift it. That's right." Encouraging, rocking. I saw horror once in a visitor's eyes. I saw the sexual seeming of this activity and I began to worry. Not now. You were seven, seven and a half, eight... but what of the future? What would happen when you were so large and lumpen that our two diminutive helpers would be unable to handle you? I had images of large Fijian women, Samoan women. We would have to move to some remote Pacific island. And how would your body seem to you with its bleedings and changing shapes? I tell you the honest truth, Stevie, I was dreading the future and the necessities it would impose. I shut my mind to these thoughts. We took each day as it came.

And I was aware too that as you grew, as you became heavier, it grew steadily harder for you to lift your head. Was it that your arms were no longer strong enough to hold you? Or were you giving up? Or...?

One day, I was walking along the path into the village when I bumped into Brenda, a neighbour. We stopped to pass the time of day. She asked after you. I said you didn't go out much but were happy in your own way.

"You know," Brenda said. "Stevie is not just important to you. She's important to the whole *gwailo* community on Cheung Chau. She is the heart of the community."

I was very struck by the thought that you were still very much in people's minds. It was true that the local community had rallied round us. There had been two spring fairs to raise money for the fledgling Down Syndrome Association. And in many other ways, when we needed something, we were helped to get it.

And, it seems, the more we didn't take you out the more you became an idea – the idea of a beautiful little girl who has suffered more than a little girl ought to suffer.

You became the invisible mascot of the community.

This matter of not taking you out. I felt that you ought to go out. That you ought to feel the sensations of motion, the breeze, the tastes and smells of the island. But Bern pointed out that you simply became unhappy and discontented. It wasn't comfortable for you. As you grew heavier it was more difficult to set you comfortably in the pushchair – I remember how you braced yourself against each movement, your eyes alert to our movements trying to guess our intention. Your feet needed to be set on the foot platform symmetrically, but somehow one always slipped off as the leg straightened as you went into your rigid 'swordsman' posture, one arm raised and your head turned to the side. I remember how I had to take hold of your foot and gently push up the toes to release the muscle catch of the knee so that it too would bend and release the other catches in the system. And the weather was always too warm or too cold, too wet or too humid.

The only time you enjoyed being in the pushchair was when

we brought you off the ferry at the cargo exit. Here wooden slats were nailed to the ramp to stop trolleys from slipping back and to give the porters friction to help them push their overloaded carts up to the top. Bump-bump-bump we would go over these slats. Bump-bump-bump. We always took them at speed. Up would go both your hands and your mouth would crack open in the widest laugh. What fun this bump-bump-bumping was.

And Patrick was so jealous of you. He would be happy in the sitting room, playing with some toy and taking no notice of anyone but if I got up and came into your room, Stevie, then quick as a flash, he would be there too smiling his engaging, impish smile. His was no sly competitiveness. Direct, honest, he would dig his way between us as I sat hugging you, rocking to the music.

I have a photo of you and Patrick posed together. Patrick has put on a false smile while you... What in any case did you know of photographs and cameras... you are sensing him near you, this strange being. You aren't frightened. There is something welcoming in your hesitant expression – a sense that you wish you understood more. Here is an energy that is more like your own energy, the energy of childhood. Looking at the photo I have the impression that you know this is your younger brother and you wish you knew more about him. But as soon as the camera is put aside Patrick is up and away.

As he grew older, he began to ask about you Stevie. He knew you were different but he couldn't explain it to himself. Or perhaps he just wanted things spoken about.

"What's wrong with Stevie?" he asked one day.

And I talked about you Stevie but how could I tell your little brother that you are brain damaged, blind, spastic, epileptic and that you have a genetic disorder known as Down's syndrome. What would that mean to him? What would it mean to anyone? Does it not make more sense to say that you are a little girl with a lot of problems and that our job is to help you? I think that's what I said to Patrick. He was only four.

There's another photograph of you. It's winter, I guess, from the dress you're wearing. From the fat you still have on you I guess too that you have not long been out of hospital. You are seated in a large black beanbag. A number of toys have been placed around you. A stuffed pig has been put by your feet. You are laughing like crazy, a big beaming, slightly piggy, laugh and there's this pig at your feet. It's almost as if there's a big piggy joke going on and you think it's the funniest thing in the whole world. And the pig does look funny tucked between your feet.

There are nights when I am awake at three or four in the morning. Are you there, God? I ask myself silently. Careful not to voice the question, careful not to seem to be asking too seriously. Are you laughing, God? Is this a game you're playing with me? And if you're playing with me, you're playing with Stevie and Bern too. Are we your playthings? Or are we acting out an archetypal drama? Or are we part of an experiment? Or are you testing us? Is there a camera in the sky capturing the daily soap of our lives? God are you there? The ultimate paranoid scenario: God is my enemy. Or is it Satan: the Job scenario? I try to balance out the evidence. I was lost and I am found. Stevie saved me. Love and pain saved me. For me the pain is good pain. For Stevie? Clearly not. Life has damaged her. She may be happy with her music and her happiness may be quite intense, as it seems to be, but we could never say that she has benefited from the pain. We could never say that there was any possibility she might overcome it, that it might have a positive value. Yet if God exists and I have an immortal soul then so does she. If life is a moral testing ground then it is so for both of us. This is the paradox: I was given pain when I needed it. My pain has been a blessing. My pain has led me to consider the idea that there is a master of all our destinies – a master that we might call God but who is no Christian God – yet, if he is the master of my fate then he is the master of Stevie's. But the pain he gave to Stevie could never be justified, not in terms of her own fate. So if God exists he is a capricious God and our fates might just as well be decided by a roll of cosmic dice. Do you hear me, God? The same logic that might lead me to believe in you as a moral guide, a moral force, forces me also to reject the possibility. Are you there, God? Are you listening? And what other pains have you got in store for me?

And so my thoughts turn at three or four in the morning.

And how are we to explain it all? If there is a purpose to life – as the theological religions assure us there is – it must – surely? – be a purpose common to us all. Both you, Stevie, and me, and everyone else. There may be many paths to the goal – as the Buddhists say – but the proper objective remains one: nirvana, heaven.

One of the possible Christian messages on this theme of life's purpose can be derived from Jesus's parable of the talents. Each man was given a different number of talents to make use of as they would and they each responded differently. It was the man who took his investment and increased its value who received Jesus's approval.

No religion is so out of touch with reality that it proclaims we all start from the same place. No. There is a fundamental unfairness. This is a given and must be accepted. All religions take this view. Fate is a random and inexplicable force and it would be silly to battle against it – or even to feel resentful.

I can certainly accept this for myself. I have been brought up with sufficiently Protestant virtues to respect the message of the talents. But, Stevie, for you, what sense can it have?

Certainly, there are times I feel my fate is unfolding like a piece of theatre, a kind of heroic tragedy. Heroic in a classical sense, reflecting the travails of an individual who embraces his fate. It seems so perfectly designed for me that I feel there is a pattern, a theme – an author.

But it does nevertheless seem strange that the pain in my life should be drawing me closer to an idea of God. Surely, pain is the ultimate disproof. If God was wholly good, the argument goes, he wouldn't have created a world filled with pain. And if he wasn't wholly good? Well then he wouldn't be God – not a Christian God. But the argument chases its own tail. God does exist – according to the protagonists of this argument – and is wholly good so how can we unravel this paradox of pain?

For myself, I can say that the pain I have been through has made me a better person. In what way? How can I explain this? I have been given something to battle with, and in battling it I have attained some victory in my own heart. I have been given love to feel, and I embrace this love with my whole soul. I was lost and I am now found. I was a piece of debris blown this way and that by contrary winds, now I am anchored solid as granite. I was lumpen, refractory, awkward, bitter, angry; now I flow with the flow of life. I have been able to embrace the pain and incorporate it into my awareness of life – even though I remain lumpen, refractory and awkward I am no longer bitter and angry. So, I can say that, for me, the pain has been good.

And, to put this on another plane of discussion, if there was no pain how could we progress in understanding throughout our lives? Without pain there could be no moral structure – no sense of right or wrong, however we apply these terms. There would be no existential meaning. So at this level, we can accept that pain fought with, felt, perhaps even overcome, is, if not a good, at least an inevitable and necessary part of existence.

But what about the pain that you, Stevie, have been through? How has it been a good for you? There is no possibility that you could ever benefit from the pain you have suffered. You have never been in a position to invest your talents wisely. But you are a soul. If God created you to undergo a travail in the valley of the shadow of life, then how did he allow you to be crippled before the starting gun was fired? There is no satisfactory Christian answer.

The Muslim answer is slightly better – if only because it expresses most clearly our ignorance: It is, simply, *Inshallah* – God's will. This is the Jewish answer too. God's management of the universe is beyond man's grasp and he cannot be called to account. It would be impertinent, even blasphemous, to question God, or God's purpose. His actions are arbitrary. This is not a God – neither Allah nor Yahweh – that we can turn to for rational explanation.

But if we push for an answer we are faced with a God of such great cruelty that he can – however inscrutably – nevertheless will a fate such as yours, Stevie, on any little boy or girl. Is this a God that we should bow down before? It seems to me – in my ignorance – that this is a God I could not worship. Even if his existence was as concrete and clear as the four walls of this room, I would turn my head away from him. And yet, from my perspective, there is a value in saying that fate is fate. We must accept what is given. The answer of Islam and Judaism has a good message for me. But it can say nothing to give value to your pain, Stevie, your suffering.

What then of the Hindu answer that this is the result of karma, of an endless succession of past lives. It's true that the idea of a series of lives lessens the horror. You did something in your previous existence to merit this suffering. I did something in my previous life to merit my pain. But who is the grand mathematician of life and death who can so subtly calculate the appropriate concurrence of fates? But even if we accept that this is done by some all-knowing impartial force, there is, in addition, the corollary that we can change our karmic future through our actions and choices in the here and now. But how could you, Stevie, exercise any choice? How could you, Stevie, change your karmic flow so that next time your life will be better? That's what I find impossible to understand.

And some, of course, object that such an explanation makes you responsible for your own pain. There is no need for us to feel pity. You have got what you cosmically deserve. But I do feel pity for you, Stevie. A great and terrible pity.

And for the Buddhist, pain is the foundation of his whole system of belief. Because there is pain, there cannot be a personal God, for no God would be so inhumane as to inflict this pain. Therefore we live in a Godless universe where pain is the law and to escape the pain is the objective. But for me, the pain has been good. Should I seek to escape it? Is there nothing good that can be said about this pain? And for you Stevie, there is no possibility that you can choose to leave the pain behind. You are held fast in the grip of pain. You cannot choose. What can Buddhism say to either of us?

The religious teacher Sri Aurobindo seeks to find a way around this problem. He suggests that God is not separate from the universe but is embodied in the universe. He therefore feels all the pain that is inflicted in the universe because he is incarnate in every single one of us. While this makes God less horrible, more sympathetic, it does not give meaning to the pain.

And what of the second or third largest religion in the world – measured by the number of adherents? I speak of the folk religion of the Chinese people. If there is wisdom here it is that there is no theology, no absolute, all powerful, supreme being, no ultimate. Pain and evil are random and haphazard events caused by evil spirits and other disharmonies, the malevolent eye of a neighbour perhaps. All one can do is manipulate the geomantic forces of nature and pray for the individual intercession of Gods or ancestors. Perhaps the problem is simply that we have not put mirrors in the correct places to reflect away these evil influences. I have statues of Gods in my house. Is this the cause of our suffering, are we being punished through you, for our elementary neglect to worship these pieces of wood and metal?

The Taoist is more philosophical and has a framework of dark and light, passive and active forces: but he has nothing of interest to say about the fate of the individual soul.

It is true our minds are too small to be able to comprehend the divine will of the cosmic soul, if there is a cosmic soul. But, Stevie, I sense that you are an affront to all religious systems.

In the end I incline to a universe devoid of cosmic purpose, a universe of meaningless, random cause and effect. A universe of accident. And as for our moral and ethical structures, we make our own moral universes as we can with the bricks at hand. We react to the pain as it suits us: stoically, with epicurean disdain, with Islamic resignation, with Buddhistic contemplation of the infinite, with Hinduistic contemplation of past aeons of cause and effect, with the embrace of Christian love or with atheistic resignation at the ultimate inevitability of personal annihilation.

In the end, Stevie, all I can say is that God – fate, what you will – made a gift of you to me and you have blessed me. I hope I have, in turn, helped you on your journey through this life. And if I am wrong, if there is an after-life, I dearly hope it is a place where you can blossom in wisdom and laughter.

There is a whole world out there Stevie. People pass along the lane outside the house. What do they know of you? More to the point, what do you know about them? Early morning, old men and women walk down to the temple to gossip and do their morning exercises at the water's edge.

The seasons change. Dry, crisp, sunny autumn changes to the hard cold of January, February warms up to the cool clammy months of March, April then fresh May gives way to June with its early hint of summer and then it's there: the sticky cauldron of July, August and then the intense, breathless heat of early September. Then one day in mid September a cool north breeze blows. I remember one year it came through at 3:10 in the afternoon – a cool breeze that takes the sting out of the heat – a blessed cool breath.

You lie there in your room, Stevie, and the seasons change around you. You don't hear the patter of feet on the dry concrete or the slip of boots on wet leaves and the silvery traces of snail trails. What are they to you? What can you know of them?

And this island of ours attracts some strange characters. There is Mr Woo. Early morning finds him running with a pack of dogs down to the beach for his morning swim. Almost feral. Morning and evening he carries a stick. He beats the fences where fenced-in dogs lather themselves up in a futile frenzy of barking. He laughs. Home for him is a burnt-out shell of a building. He lives among piles of rubbish. The day it burnt, it was already in flames when he returned home. He just stood there and laughed. He didn't even ask if his mother was OK. As it happened she was. He moved to the ruin across the path where he fixed up the kitchen as their living space. His mother followed without complaint. And he quotes Shakespeare and reads the Bible and every day he goes into the city to the music library to listen to Beethoven and Handel and Mozart and all the rest of them. He goes with a bamboo pole over his shoulder carrying his daily needs: a flask of soup, some scraps of food, a roll of newspaper to lay out should he feel like lying down. And people in the village pass on their hand-me-downs so there are days when he looks positively natty. It amuses him to wear a herring-bone jacket with a tie as he pokes through the dustbins outside the City Hall.

There is Mrs Wong who can be seen at five in the morning pushing a cart filled with thrown-out pieces of furniture that she is rescuing. The path to her house is walled by the rubbish she has collected. Always smiling, she waddles around the island. There is something wrong with her hip. She is always happy. One day I found her at the top of my lane. There was a village cart on which she had laid some cardboard sheets. An old man was lying on the cardboard. She too laid down next to him: to keep him company, to keep him warm.

There is the self-made artist, Ah-Sing, who cleared a square of unused ground and fenced it in with the metallic detritus of our times: bicycle wheels, tin trays, rusty colanders, the insides of washing machines. He made it perfect and then it bored him and the grass has taken over again.

There's a world out there, Stevie. A world that you could never know. And the world knows so little of you. I need to tell them about you.

Hips. I can't remember now what the problem was but we were referred to the doctor who deals with these things. I think it was that we had been told there was a danger your hip bones would come out of the sockets. The doctor checked you and X-rays confirmed the fears.

"Both the hip bones have been pulled out of the hip sockets by the spasticity of the muscles," he explained. "You can see here, and here," he pointed at the X-ray, "that they've been like that for a long time. They've ground into the pelvic bone."

Bern and I looked at each other. More problems. More decisions. More hospitals. This sounded bad.

"The problem is that the muscles are so tight they are pulling the bones out."

"So she needs an operation?"

"Well, one option would be to reset the hips in the sockets. We'd have to do one at a time. She would be immobilised for about six weeks. And even then there's a very good chance they'd just come out again."

"So it's hardly worth it."

"Not really. There's no hope that she'll ever be able to walk on her own. So, no. She's in no discomfort."

"It won't cause her any problems?"

"No. The only thing you have to make sure is that you keep exercising her legs so that they don't tighten up at the top. If that happens we'll have to cut one of the tendons. That's so you can keep her clean."

Thank God we got the straight picture from this doctor. Two years later another doctor told us your hip bones were out of the sockets and that the only way to rectify it was to put you into hospital and do things to you. He left that thought hanging in the air.

"But it's not really necessary is it?" I said.

He thought about for a long moment and then conceded that it probably wasn't necessary.

We saved you a little pain, Stevie. We saved all of us a little pain.

There was a lot of pain over those years, the constant underlying pain and the continuing new pains that added to the burden of pain. We felt this pain differently, Bern and I. It drove us into ourselves. And of course the pain was there all the time so we became numb to it and all we could set ourselves to doing was the dull task of keeping going. And when I think about it I feel so sorry.

According to the theory of acupuncture, there are channels of subtle energy that run up and down the body. These channels, called meridians, connect such disparate parts of the body as ear and knee, heart and big toe and so on. Along each meridian there are points which act as gateways or boosters. The health of the system can be maintained by putting energy in or taking energy out using these points.

I believe a deep relationship is like a body, energy channels run between the two people. The health of the system requires that living energy runs freely along these meridians. But the energy can become blocked, silted up, imbalanced. Maybe it gets detoured, dispersed.

Something like that happened with Bern and me, Stevie. She's with you now so she can tell you her side of things. There were blockages, imbalances. We became closed off from each other. Not all the time, but enough of the time. We stopped feeding each other, became a drain on each other, a subtle stultifying of the subtle energy. We did our own things in our own time separately with separate groups of friends. I remember nights of lying in silent agony wanting to bridge the gap that had grown between us. I wanted to reach out and... what? What could I say? How could I explain the blank, sickening, neutered chaos of my feelings? I didn't know and so I didn't do anything – just wrestled with my unhappiness. For months and years. I thought of divorce, but that was not an option while you were alive. Together we could cope. Apart…? It didn't bear thinking of.

And maybe Bern felt the same way.

And there was another aspect to it. While you were alive, we occupied a space called 'Now'. The past slipped away in the jet stream, the future flowed into us, was with us and was gone, but we could only focus on this present moment that wrapped around us. We put aside no savings, we had no money to put aside, and I didn't even think of it. This wasn't a problem for me. I felt secure. I had you. I had Bern. Yes, despite everything she was the rock of my life. But I was not the rock of hers. She tried to focus on the coming future, tried to find some sense of a future stability. She wanted to buy a house. But every time she found one she wanted something went wrong. The price moved, or someone made a higher bid or she hesitated. I think that hurt her. She had the sense to see we were hurtling towards a future that we had not secured in any way. I was too focused on the present to be a support to her. Looking back, with hindsight, it is perhaps no wonder that something snapped.

There is a view that cancer is a disease of the spirit.

Your mother, Mummy, Bern was such a person who gave of herself – gave to everyone – gave so much that she grew tired of giving – but always refused to receive. She refused even birthday gifts, saying they were a waste of money. And I did not have the eyes to see.

If you ask me, I say this is what happened. In some corner of her unconscious some switch was clicked on by a deep nameless subterranean void of the soul that we call despair.

Or was it, I think, hoping to excuse myself, that her habit of sitting with shoulders hunched meant that she became a shallow breather, which in turn affected the oxygenation of her body's tissues which in turn encouraged the development of cancer cells, as another theory has it?

Or did I infect her with a virus?

Or was it diet? Or chemical poisoning? Radon seeping into the house from the crumbling granite beneath us?

Whatever the cause, Bern discovered she had cancer in the spring of 1994.

The archaeology of memories: sometimes we step painfully on the fragmentary images, pottery shards of the long gone and irredeemable past, that, for whatever odd chemical reason, our brains have chosen to allow selective recall.

Once, in Bali, in a moment of exuberance, Bern hugged my arm and said to me: "Jonathan, you are really wonderful."

Is that not a wonderful thing to hear? We had passed through a low point in our relationship and perhaps she saw this on my face. She wanted to cheer me up. She wanted to change the energy. But I was stuck in the swamp of depression, perhaps, to dignify it with a name, but I could not take hold of my feelings and shake them as I wanted to. I wanted to say to Bern: "And you are wonderful too." I wanted to. The words were there to say, and the mind was prompting it, but somehow I could not bring myself to say them. If I regret anything at all it is that I did not hug her at the moment and say with full conviction: "And you are wonderful too, Bern."

Oh Stevie, more than anything else in the whole world, more than any other action I have taken or not taken in the snaking path of the past, I regret this.

The first sign of the cancer was bleeding that began one October. She went to see a doctor who did a Pap smear. Calling up, later, for the results she was told, by a nurse, they were negative. Just a normal everyday consultation. But the bleeding continued and the cancerous cells that were there grew undisturbed.

Later, when it was much too late, we got a copy of the results. Yes, there was a tick against the item 'negative for malignancy' – but a handwritten note at the bottom mentioned the presence of abnormal cells.

But Bern wasn't told this.

The result also suggested that she be re-tested in six months time. But Bern wasn't told this.

The doctor herself made a note to herself to retest at the time of the next visit.

Bern wasn't told this. Later, at the next visit, no further test was done.

It is well-known that Pap smear tests have only a 70% reliability rating at best.

But Bern wasn't told this, not until much later when she was told they were not one hundred percent reliable.

If she had been told any of these things she would certainly have requested a new test.

Not that a new test should have been necessary, for when the original slide was seen by two other experienced pathologists much later, they stated that the slides showed clear signs of cancer. The slide had been misread. Apparently, this is common.

Bern didn't know this until it was much too late.

Three months later, in extreme pain and serious discomfort, she returned to see the same doctor who after giving her a quick inspection gave her some antibiotics. No new Pap smear test was made.

Two months later Bern attended a different clinic. They found clear signs of cancer that had already spread. She was rushed into hospital.

When she first heard the news Bern rang the first doctor.

"They've found cancer."

"Oh!" Business-like. "I'll check your records and call you back."

When she called back, she admitted with some embarrassment that the original results did mention the presence of odd-shaped cells.

"Why didn't you tell me?"

I can picture Bern hanging on to the telephone line listening in dumb nausea to the silence at the other end. Inside her own head she is screaming furious invective at this... this... idiot who told her not to worry, to take some antibiotics, to rest and take it easy... her mouth thick with disgust, raging with a nauseous, impotent, bitter fury. Let us stay with this moment a while longer. This question "why didn't you tell me?" echoing in the chambers of her mind. Perhaps, more than anything, feeling incomprehension. She had paid to have professional diagnosis, to have tests done. The tests were done and yet she was not told the results. Not talked through the significance of every last detail. Medicine on the run. And the cost? Her life. Death stares back at her in the gloom of the pay-phone cubicle. The extra pain and damage of late treatment. She can feel from the other end of the line the waves of bleak wordless embarrassment wanting the call to end. End. End. And feeling sick to her soul, Bern replaces the receiver.

At first it was hoped that surgery would solve the problem but there were already the early signs of possible if not imminent spread beyond the uterus. A course of radiation and chemotherapy was planned. What alternative did we have? What did we know? Of course we agreed. Like lambs to the slaughter.

It was at this time that a young doctor, in all innocence, suggested that the hospital have a look at the original slide to see what changes had occurred in the meantime. And so we obtained the slide, had it retested and discovered the negligence of the second doctor. The cancer cells were clearly visible.

What? A second shrill silent scream of dull impotent rage. What!!??

How could there be so much fucking (sorry, Stevie) negligence in the world?

I immediately set out to read what I could about cancer. The local cancer society had a small library and I plunged into it headlong. I had supposed there was a consensus. I was quickly disabused. I discovered facts that made paranoia reasonable. There were men whose careers had been destroyed because they had claimed to have a cure for cancer: Max Gerson, a German Jewish doctor who claimed to cure cancer with a special diet; an American inventor Raymond Rife who had invented a machine that zapped the microbe he said caused cancer. There were scientific giants like

Linus Pauling who were side-lined by the establishment because they proposed that vitamin C in large quantities – ten or more grams a day, twenty, even thirty – could cure cancer. There were herbalists who were hauled in and out of court because they claimed herbs could cure cancer. And this was in America, the land of freedom and democracy. (An America also that is prey to the digital opposition of black and white, God and Satan, decency and communism, a McCarthyite streak that still stains the national psyche. But an America too where individuals of great honesty and integrity have stood up well against the power of big business and the corrupt federal agencies who work hand-in-pocket with it.)

Scientists who claimed there was another, as yet unrecognised, vitamin – one they called B17 and which was found in large quantities in almonds and apricot pits, that was a potent anti-cancer weapon if combined with vitamin A and enzymes – lost their research grants. Scientists who could demonstrate cancer tumours shrinking through obscure and complex processes were forced to flee to the Bahamas to continue their work.

Was it really true that doctors were struck off for dispensing vitamins? Was that credible? Of course it was not credible. Not in a rational universe, not in a sensible society. But apparently it happened all the time in America. This was one of the things I was discovering. I read Ralph Moss's book that documented this process: *The Cancer Industry*. I read other books too: books that said diet, herbs, supplements (some I'd never heard of: co-enzyme Q10?), oxygen, magnets, homoeopathy, shark cartilage and diluted papaya leaf tea. These books didn't talk, they shouted, yelled, screamed and stomped their feet in rage. I began to get a sense of dislocation, fragmentation. Later, much later, it began to come together. But it was too late. Always too late. Always the sense that if only one had known that fact two, three weeks ago, decisions might have been different. Always the sense of being wrong-footed.

Then there were the chapters here, the quotes there, the odd scientifically established fact somewhere else that attacked the use of radiation (it was damaging, it could make the tumour more aggressive), the use of chemotherapy (it was damaging, extremely so when coupled with radiation, and it didn't work for 95% of cancers, many of which it was nevertheless prescribed for) and even surgery.

Oh Stevie! It was now that the silence and distrust that had grown between us betrayed its bitter fruit. It was one thing for me to read these books, it was another to convince Bern that there was another route that we should be exploring. She placed her trust in the doctors. She refused to hear anything against radiation. She determined to pursue chemotherapy. She refused to take the herbs I bought – where's the sell-by date? she asked derisively. Are you a doctor? How can you believe what you read? People can write anything. (Yes, Bern, but so many books?)

And so she persevered with the radiation – six weeks; and the chemotherapy – one day a month. They tired her out but actually she seemed to cope quite well with the chemotherapy, a day or two of extreme-tapering-to-slight nausea. It wasn't good for her to be in crowds, she became tired of travelling (tired also perhaps of the arguments we were having) and your aunt Martha was able to make the foods she preferred, the bird's nest soup, the bitter melon, and brother-in-law Alan would practice his Chi-Kung and his massage on her. Our friend Françoise was there to drive her to and from hospital. So, for perhaps ten days a month, Bern effectively moved away from home to Martha and Alan's flat.

She put on a brave face and we all coped as well as we could with the new arrangements. Her hair fell out and although friends banded together and bought her a wig, she never did wear it, preferring instead the elegant dash of a bright scarf or a light blue beret.

Everything seemed to be going well. The markers – the chemicals in the urine that indicated the presence of cancer – were undetectable. Her blood counts were good. Then she had the fifth chemo session and it knocked her into a state of vicious nausea and weakness and pain. There was only one more session to go but she refused even to contemplate it. Two doctors screamed at her that she had to do it but she insisted I tell them that she wasn't going to – she said it as placatingly as she could but she had had enough.

Ah Stevie! Stevie! Life doesn't stand still.

It started as it had done the other times. A raised temperature that wouldn't come down. Difficulty breathing. No, I said. She'll be OK. Stevie's a fighter. Let's see how she is tomorrow.

The third day Del and Lyn looked serious.

"She's not well."

It was only three or four months since the last time you'd been in hospital. Each stay threatened to be for weeks or months at a time. I was prepared to be responsible but Del wasn't. Lyn wasn't. I couldn't make them. I could feel the whole weight of the household waiting for me to say the words.

"OK. Get ready."

I remember the ferry trip, Stevie. You weren't well and you lay slumped in my arms. You were heavy. Even now I retain a physical memory of the feeling of your weight in my arms as I hug you as I sometimes still do, hugging space as I cradle the memory of you in my arms.

At the hospital they told us what we already knew. Pneumonia. Viral pneumonia. There was little they could do. Antibiotics of course. Though it wasn't bacterial, there might be bacterial involvement. And X-rays. Every day. And we were there because we wanted to hand over the responsibility of care to someone else. And they pumped you full of antibiotics because they couldn't just do nothing. And they gave you X-ray after X-ray, dangerous though that was, because they had to measure the advance or retreat of the illness. They were doctors. This was a hospital. Those were their tools. We had brought you in. We were ultimately responsible. I'm sorry Stevie.

And it didn't go well. The virus was winning. You were having problems breathing so a perspex box was placed over your head and oxygen pumped in so that you were breathing a richer mixture.

I had just read a book suggesting that vitamin C in large doses had a strong anti-viral effect. I talked this over with the doctor. Do you have suppositories or can we give her some vitamin C intravenously? I asked him. He looked at me strangely. What kind of crank was he dealing with? I lent him the book. He came back an hour later and shook his head.

"Look, none of these articles are by Professors of Medicine. They're just biochemists or general practitioners. My team would just laugh at me if I suggested it."

"It might work. Surely we should try everything."

"I'll tell you frankly, I don't know anything about vitamins. We don't study this in medical school. The last time I heard of vitamins was in biology at school."

"But, as an experiment. It wouldn't hurt. There would be no harm in it."

"I couldn't do it." The doctor smiled apologetically. "In any case we don't stock that kind of thing in the pharmacy."

The first day we talked about it, we did so in an easy-going way. It was the talk of intelligent people. Abstract. But the next day, Stevie, your condition was worse and causing concern. I decided to act. I went to a health shop where I bought some vitamin C crystals. Del and I mixed them with juice and made you drink it. There was nothing you could do about it. It went down a tube they had threaded through your nose into your stomach.

The next day I came in early to see you. The doctor was on his rounds but when he saw me, he signalled that he needed to talk to me.

"I haven't seen her this morning but I've had the results. I'm afraid it looks bad. The infection has gone out of control. I'm very sorry. I'll be along in half an hour. We'll talk about what we can do then."

Oh God! I hurried to your room. You had been allocated your own room so that Del and Lyn could take it in turns to use the other bed so that you always had someone at hand.

"How is she? The doctor says..."

I stopped. Del was smiling. She may have been feeding you some congee. You were sitting propped up.

"She's much better today."

I could see that.

"I'll go and tell the doctor."

I went over to him and told him you were looking well.

He looked at me with a grim expression.

"I'm afraid the tests show her condition is very bad. We'll talk in a while. First I have to see these other patients."

Sometime later he came in and explained about the test results.

"But just look at her, doctor," we protested. "She looks well."

He paused. The evidence of the tests was too strong in his mind but after ten or fifteen minutes he took your temperature. He looked thoughtful.

"Yes, she does seem better."

As I was leaving at the end of the visit he stopped me.

"The tests," he said. "I think there was an error. It happens. It's what we call a false positive."

"It could have been the vitamin C."

"No, almost certainly, it was a false positive."

Maybe, Stevie, but I don't believe it.

And the virus did leave but the pneumonia had weakened your lungs. You were never able to leave the oxygen for long. You started to turn blue. But you had beaten the pneumonia again. It would be only a matter of time before we had you home again. Or so we hoped for a few days, a week. But then, more and more, we started to look at the machine beside your bed. The numbers on it hovered, at first, in the early hundreds.

"This measures her tissue oxygen levels," the nurse explained.

If it dropped below a pre-set level an alarm would go off and in theory nurses would come running.

One day the level plummeted from 97 to 24 in seconds. We grabbed you, lifted you up, patted your back, pleaded with you – Steevie!! – and it slowly rose again.

You had needles permanently set in your arm, kept in place by tape so that drugs could be quickly and efficiently administered. Each position would last a day or two before ceasing to be any use. It wasn't easy to find a new vein – there were many failed attempts. Your arm was a mass of bruises.

But there were moments, days, when you were your old self. Your rabbity skewed yellow stub teeth revealed by lips peeled back with laughter and joy at the music. Your mews of thoughtful puzzlement. Your open-mouthed pleasure and your dancing glistening eyes. You were a fighter. You were a survivor. But the numbers on the oxygen machine were coming down and the nurses were resetting the level at which the alarm went off. Always down. And one half of us understood that this meant you were dying but that word was never uttered. Not by the doctor. Not between us. But we all knew. And we all rejected the knowledge.

Then there was the day you slept all day without waking. And the three days you were awake and sleep wouldn't come to you and the doctor refused to give you any sedation saying it might kill you.

We rubbed your back constantly, pushing you to one side, then another. You were moved and pushed and exercised as much as you could tolerate. And the oxygen level came down through the seventies and the sixties. The oxygen tube gushed oxygen into your nose and still the numbers dropped. The virus returned. It went from one lung to the other. You were pumped full of every antibiotic they could think of – even for AIDS-related pneumonia.

One day two oxygen taps were full on and you were obviously, very obviously dying – then next morning you only needed one and you were stable and awake and laughing. The day before the day you slept 24 hours (death coma?) you had been giggling. We felt useless. We held you by your flaccid hands hoping you felt some of our love and concern. From time to time you heaved your two arms apart in the air as though struck by some sudden appreciation, a newly obvious truth.

And still you didn't die.

It was strange to be alone in the house. Indeed I felt half a stranger in this space – trespassing its hidden boundaries. An empty home has no welcome in it, no bustle. But still... still... to be alone, all alone by myself. How long had it been? I savoured the feeling.

I took my shoes off. This was the house rule. Peeled off my socks. Threw them in the corner of the room where the wicker washing basket stood. A beer followed by another beer followed by a beer? Whisky? The evening stretched ahead. A dark tunnel of time.

I showered. The house felt very empty. I walked around it luxuriating in my nakedness. With three women around most of the time, this was a rare luxury. And the house was filled with absent sounds: Patrick jumping on the cushions playing with a toy in his hand, muttering strange narratives to himself. Dialogues of impending but escaped-just-in-time dooms. Bern's complainings and insistences: do this, do that. And the soft whir of the cassette from your room – songs I never seemed to tire of, songs that were your salvation. Poor Stevie. It was always poor Stevie. A sigh.

The house was empty. You were in hospital with Del and Lyn looking after you. Patrick was with a friend and Bern was at her sister's. Peace and quiet, I thought to myself, savouring the prospect. An evening of solitude. An evening of no one else at all.

I dried myself off and put on a sarong and a holey T-shirt that Bern kept meaning to throw out but somehow returned washed and ironed even. Having two domestic helpers helped. All I had to do was continue to be able to afford it as long as Stevie... There was nothing much saved but still I could just manage. I sometimes wondered what would have happened if ever I had not been able to cope financially – what might still happen... I put the thought aside.

There was a moon up, not yet full but more than half – a pregnant moon. It illumined the bay below. By the light I could see the exposed sand and rocks below. The tide was out. There were advantages in overlooking a rocky bay – not so many people came to use it. Not at night anyway. The steep, narrow, overhung, disintegrating path that led down to it was no encouragement. But the blackness of the sky remained implacable. Neither clouds nor stars – a jet black firmament. Maybe later there would be stars. Twinkle twinkle...

It was still. Perfect end-of-September weather. I could sit out on the balcony and watch the lights string across the horizon. Fishing boats. Across on the next island a cluster of lights where ten years ago there were none – a whole town had sprung up. China. There was a boat in the bay too. A small sampan stringing out a net, a light hanging over the end. Damn! I slapped at my leg and hit the mosquito that had just jabbed me. I turned from the view and went back indoors.

Yes, it was very quiet. Some music perhaps. Some music that would go with the silence and the solitude. Gamelan? The scintillating sounds of Mr Sharma's Santoor? The santoor – a dulcimer – a hundred-stringed instrument hit with soft mallets. *The Scintillating Sounds of...* That was the title. Indian corn. But the music. That was something else. The wonders of compact discs. The music of the world in every home. Undramatic music. That's what I wanted. Music that would bring an edge of life into the room, no more.

And Stevie, you were dying... And the evening and the solitude were endless and I was so terribly alone.

Oh Stevie... Eight and a half years old. You had been through so much and now you were dying. Probably. Possibly. I hoped so. This couldn't go on. How much longer could I go on half-wishing you would die and half-wishing you could come home and be all right again? This halfway house of contradictory emotions was too much to bear.

It was now clear to us that you were going to die soon. But it was a clear truth that we preferred not to look straight in the face. You would fight for a few days and then spend a day almost comatose from exhaustion. Was this it? But no! The next day, refreshed, you came back to almost your best. But then the next day, you were exhausted again. The monitor measuring the oxygen levels of your blood showed the steady decline. 80 became 65 became 48. Down it dropped. How much further could it drop? And we saw these numbers and we ignored their significance. They were just numbers. Just numbers (But they were the measure of your life!)

But of course a miracle might occur. You had fought back from the brink of death before. You could come back to us and life would go on as it did before. But we accepted now that you were going to die and I, I can't speak for Bern, but I wanted an end to the long drawn-out agony of your suffering. It just went on and on. But, I said to you in my mind, sweetheart, take your time. I don't want to rush you. If you are prepared to fight then I am too. Your life has completed its mission, the cycle of purpose. You've done your job. If you want to go then go in peace. Please God it is easy.

And I felt so mean and despicable: a man who wants his daughter to die!

And I love you so much.

And as I write this four years later I have tears streaming helplessly from my eyes.

The last time I saw you alive was the night before. I had stayed with you for half an hour or so and was about to leave when the cassette started to play 'Twinkle twinkle little star'. I waited till the end. I hoped this would be it, the poetically appropriate close – and it was.

Then, that last night of your life, I took Bern out to see a concert of Irish music. The Chieftains were in town and I had good tickets. It was a joyous evening for the crowd and there was a girl with magical long legs dancing Irish jigs. And I think Bern may have got some pleasure from it. I hope so. She was suffering badly and moved with arthritic slowness. It wasn't often these last few months we had gone out to enjoy ourselves – even the last few years. Somehow we had put ourselves on the sidelines. We had not paid enough attention to having a night out. Having fun. Just the two of us. So I had got the tickets some weeks before. And so we watched the Chieftains and enjoyed ourselves knowing that, Stevie, you were going to die the next day, or the day after. It could not be long now. And we sat and watched the Chieftains and tried to escape this awful awful present.

After the concert I took Bern to her sister's flat and then went home.

The call came in the morning.

"Come. Quick." Lyn's unusually clear and unambiguous message. 9:15. I could just make the hovercraft if I hurried. I dispensed with shaving. It was 10:30 when I got to the ward. I saw the matron gesture with her eyes to the doctor, who turned to intercept me. This doctor was not afraid to talk, to say what had to be said, to name the unnameable.

"I'm afraid she's gone. She died peacefully. I've phoned her mother. She took it calmly."

"Thank you," I mumbled. "We know you did everything…"

"Please…" shaking his head as if to say: let's dispense with that conversation now. There are more important things to say, to think. "Sit with her for a while. I'll come later. There are some formalities."

Of course.

I nodded and continued to the room where you lay so still and stiff. I had been waiting for this death. Wanting it. Wanting the end of the not knowing, but knowing that if it wasn't this time it would be the next and not having the strength for it to go on and on as it had seemed possible it might. But the shock of your dear, lifeless body was wholly unexpected. The tears coursed down my face. You lay flat on the bed, eyes open a crack, your mouth open as it always had been open. Only the energy had gone.

"Oh Stevie. Oh sweetheart!"

Del made space for me as I bent down to kiss the soft, still warm, still soft, hands and cheeks. You were a touch yellower than normal but it was really only the immobility that was new. Your hands were still soft and warm – warm from Del's holding them, I guessed. Your cheek was cool as I pressed my own wet cheek against it.

"Oh sweetheart." I said and kissed your forehead.

Your eyes still open a fraction.

Here was the mystery that it was impossible to learn at second hand. Stevie. You had gone and left behind this body of flesh. But you, the person, had gone. Where to? Lifted as a spirit to Heaven? Oh the comfort of religions that held that the energy remained coherent and was not scattered to the cosmos. Or was life like a shrivelled seed gone into hibernation deep inside? Oh dear Stevie!

"How was it?"

Del's eyes were dark with tears. She spoke to me: "She wanted to die last night. She stopped breathing for a moment. About three o'clock. But I said to her: Oh darling! Don't go now. Your daddy is coming in the morning. He wants to say goodbye to you. And she came back and she kept going until eight o'clock and I said to her please, darling. Keep going. Your daddy is coming. Please wait to say goodbye. I thought you were coming in early. And then Lyn came and she said you weren't coming until later and she didn't have the energy to stay any longer. Her eyes had been half closed like this but suddenly her eyes opened wide" – those white luminous eyes that I would never see again – "her chest went like this, on the right side..." – she mimed a shudder – "and then she seemed to accept it and she became very peaceful and the monitor just dropped to zero..."

And my tears flowed as I contemplated the thought that you, Stevie, had waited for me and in the end I had not been there. Mute, nameless needs as fundamental as to have your hands in mine when you died... You could only gesture with the flutter of your living spirit. The poetic force of this last sad twist in the story over-rode all the mean thoughts that slowly sought to modify the verdict. Had you really waited for me? Had you ever really known who daddy was? Oh Stevie. Blessed are you. You remained pure. Happiness and pain – pure and absolute. In you, there were no grey areas, no subtle contradictions of feeling. And I wanted to pick you up and hug you and crush you to my chest. A hug. Even such a simple act. This was always beyond you. You could not hug. I remember the weight of you in my arms. For months afterwards I would hold my arms out and make as if I were rocking you on my lap, and I could make believe I could feel your floppy weight against my arms, against my shoulder, your arms slipping awkwardly over my shoulder. But you liked to be hugged. And your face would crack open in a wild, unflattering, glorious grimace of silent laughter. Not now, of course. Now, your face remained uncharacteristically still. And how do you say goodbye to a person who has died? Who is no longer there? The cassette was still playing softly, in case you were still there listening in some deep recess of the mind. The mystery. Was your spirit hovering, showering benedictions on us all? For you would have forgiven me for being late and missing your death – not being there to say the last goodbye when the last goodbye would have meant something. Your love was absolute. Or had your spirit travelled up that long corridor to the light beyond, the light that those who returned from death have reported? It would be so nice to have a Heaven like an English country estate on a fine English summer's day – a nursing home for the spirit bruised by life – far better than the Heaven where everyone went about constantly praising the Lord, as one minister at one funeral I had been to had described it.

And there was the matter of the funeral. I would find no solace in Christian or Buddhist rituals. I had it in mind to sit on a beach with some friends present and after a while to scatter your ashes over the rocks and the sea of the bay below the room where you had spent your life. Not just a mourning. A celebration too. A moment of keen remembrance before you dissolved in the alchemy of time. Let the sea take you away. Let the wind blow you away. But these thoughts were not for now.

The room was still. We sat in silence, waterlogged in teary

feelings, holding your hand, rubbing your tummy, rubbing fingers along scars, stroking your cheek.

"She fought hard," I said, for something to say.

Del nodded and brought her finger to Stevie's cold lips. I saw what I hadn't seen before: a blister.

"She bit her lips. She had a spasm near the end..."

I winced. Oh Stevie! Oh sweetheart!

"But in the end she was peaceful. You said she was peaceful?"

Del nodded: "Yes, she accepted it. She couldn't fight any more. She wanted to die at three o'clock..."

"Yes, you said." I had missed your death just as I had missed your birth. Such sad symmetry.

Bernadette came with Françoise. They kissed you, Stevie, with soft solicitude. Françoise unsure, not wishing to impose but feeling the full shock of death. There is no impact quite like that you get from seeing the new corpse of the loved child. The matron came with a piece of paper that outlined the procedures. Certificates had to be obtained. Registration had to be done. There was a call to the office that had to be made. I left Del to tell the story again. The doctor intercepted me on my return from the pay-phone.

"You see, they still don't really know how she died. It would be instructive. There are many things they might learn..." A post-mortem? For me, I didn't mind but I would have to ask Bern.

"No," vehemently, "She's had enough. She's been cut enough. Let her lie here in peace."

Yes.

The doctor understood: "Please don't worry. I will sign the death certificate now." Later I saw that the time of death was 9:15.

Lyn used the lip-salve to dress your lips. In life as in death. A stream of thin, pink blood erupted suddenly from your left nostril and down your cheek. We were suddenly concerned that the body was decaying but, later, the doctor said that wasn't it. It was probably an injury from the last suctioning, the last attempt to keep you alive. Even after death, you were bleeding from your wounds. Oh Stevie! Oh sweetheart! Life wasn't fair, was it?

You were wearing a pink short-sleeve shirt, red, flowery trousers and red socks.

"We cleaned her up," Del swallowed, "These are all new." Her words came out half throttled. "We cleaned her up and put a clean nappy on." Her voice cracked. She just managed to get the words out before the tears fell again.

And when is it time to say it is time to go? To say goodbye and leave, for the last time the body that is still fresh in its death – not yet frozen and embalmed into a stiff mockery of the human being who had once lived within the walls of this flesh?

And then at twelve, the matron popped her head around the corner. "I'm sorry, we need..."

The room. New lives. New occupants. The nurses had all been very kind. It was time to go.

One by one we gave you a last hug and kiss and let ourselves out from your presence.

"The cassette player, Del," I reminded, for she had been going to leave it behind so that the music would continue to play into the vast emptiness of your ears and the vast silence of the cosmos to which you had gone. We left slowly, going with our love and our grief and our regret and our sad burden of relief.

"I was going to leave it for her..."

"Don't worry, Del. She's gone now. She's gone."

The death of a child is a very hard thing.

And it stayed with me all that week as a refrain: you had hung on till nine o'clock when I would normally have arrived. And I hadn't come and you hadn't the strength to continue. I wasn't there, Stevie, I'm so sorry. But I know you will have forgiven me. I know that in your great sadness you would, if only you could, have hugged me as hard as I would have hugged you. It will stay as a reproach and a regret to my dying day – for my sake not for yours, because you will, I know, have forgiven me.

We sat with you till midday barely able to comprehend that the life had gone out of you. You looked so mute and vulnerable: in the end as you were in the beginning.

I wrote this obituary.

Stevie died at 9:15 in the morning of October 11th. She had gone into hospital because of a viral infection in her lungs and although she appeared to win that battle, she was never able to regain her independence from oxygen support. Breathing became more and more difficult – and eventually, she died from exhaustion. She fought a good fight and she died with dignity.

Stevie was eight and a half years old when she died. Most of her life she was blind, suffered from epileptic seizures and was physically unable to support herself, let alone sit or stand. These were the results of the brain damage she suffered at the age of six months, two days after an operation to correct a heart defect common to children with Down Syndrome.

So, was her life worth living? All I can say is that she would have said 'YES!' if she had the choice. She was always happy – except when she was annoyed that she didn't have her great pleasure in life – music. She loved her music. And it was this love that showed that her mental potential was perhaps greater than her physical handicaps allowed her to express. She would often signal that a cassette tape needed to be turned over, even before it had finished playing on one side. She also loved to be talked to, and have her ears kissed. These would make her break into the broadest, most beautiful smiles anybody has ever smiled. Her happiness was a miracle to see.

And for us, was her life worth living? Again we would shout 'YES!' What Stevie did for us can never adequately be described. I like to say that she broke open my heart and the love and hurt and pity flowed out and I could never close it again and so the love and hurt and pity keep on flowing out and I can't stop it. Everyone who came close to Stevie was touched by her ability to make people love her. All the carers who have lived with us, helping to look after her: Mary, Daisy, Del and Lyn – they all deeply loved Stevie. She was a sweetheart. She was an angel.

The Hong Kong Down Syndrome Association is her child. It is her gift. She gave us the strength to help build it from nothing to the very important and useful organisation it has become today.

Oh dear Stevie. We miss you and we will miss you forever.

This was your life, Stevie. It was often hard to live through, yet, I would go through it all again.

There is a passage that I would like to quote. It can be found in a book called *The World of Nigel Hunt* written by an intelligent teenage boy with Down Syndrome. He is describing a moment on a day when he was in London.

I asked the policeman when the band will be along and he said, "ten and a half minutes". So I stood and waited for at least one and a half minutes. I heard a terrific throb and my ears were lifted and with a Biff biff bang the band came along, and when they turned the corner up came their oompahs and the miserable trombones and blowed me in the middle of nowhere.

Stevie, you blowed me in the middle of nowhere.

And Louise – who so often came to sit with you in your room and coo in your ear – wrote this to me about you:

What can I say? Stevie, my Stevie. That's what I used to say. The first time I saw her. In intensive care. Tubes and wires and so still. So small. Later – out of hospital – on your shoulder, in Bern's arms. On your knee being bounced. 'You have to have a girl on your knee on a Saturday night.' Lucky Stevie.

I'd visit many evenings. My need, not yours. But I was useful – Bern could go to the bedroom with the newspaper knowing I'd keep you chatting and you'd look after Stevie. One evening, you said: 'She's blind.' How can you bear it? You can't bear it. But, it still goes on. Bern was stoical and exhausted. When the first strain eased a few years later – when you had help and Stevie had stabilised – Bern was a revelation to me: her style, her clothes, her smile. But when I first knew her – always the same clothes, the same look of utter fatigue. She never slept well did Bern, and when Stevie was little she hardly slept at all.

And you, Jonathan? I tried to look after you. Daft really. You were so tired. But noble somehow. Through some very dodgy times afterwards, I never lost that sense of you. You could walk into a room and change the atmosphere. You may always have had that power but I think it's more likely Stevie gave it to you.

Stevie. I remember her in the centre of a wide double bed. Twinkle twinkle little star. Now I know my ABC. Happy little songs. Smile Stevie smile. Blow in your ear. Make a farting noise. Or pop my finger. Stee-vee. STEE-veee. The funny things I said to her.

She was one of the first people I met in Hong Kong – just after her operation. I saw her a lot and I grew very attached to her. But I also felt very anguished for her and for you and Bern because in those days after the operation she wasn't a happy baby.

As the months went by though, she got better and stronger, and one day I was watching Bern bounce her and – she smiled. 'She smiled!' I said, and you said oh yes she quite often does that now. I was thrilled. You were both delighted of course, but for you it was wonderful but familiar, you had your smiling little girl back again. But I hadn't known Stevie happy, and as I was to find out, a happy Stevie was the true Stevie.

Her joy was infectious. It was wonderful when I got her to smile, which I learned to do quite successfully. And I remember, Jonathan, you holding her while talking about something, and laughing, and your laughter transferred to Stevie who began chuckling, till eventually we were all in fits. In later years it was harder, for me at least, to elicit that response, but all the more rewarding when I did.

I can't really articulate what I felt about Stevie, or rather, why I felt it. I tried once when a friend in England who hadn't met her was asking me about her. 'What can she do?' Not a lot really. 'Does she know who you are?' I feel as if she does but I'm not sure. Probably not. My friend was a bit puzzled. She could understand that I was fond of Stevie, but not the intensity of my affection.

I couldn't explain except to say that Stevie was herself, handicaps and all – a compelling, joyous and very loveable person.

Talking to my friend also made me realise that I didn't feel sorry for Stevie any more. Yes, she had severe limitations. But it seemed to me that they didn't bother her – she wasn't aware of other options, or frustrated that she couldn't take them. Within those limits she was as happy and contented as she could be.

What I did feel relieved and thankful about was that she managed to find the right parents and you found the right carers. I've read heart-breaking stories about children similar to Stevie who didn't have her luck. She was in the right place with the right people, and her room was the still centre of a busy household. She couldn't have been out in the hubbub of Bern's animated phone life, your jazz or Patrick aka Batman. But go into her room, a haven, tranquil, her music playing quietly and Stevie listening to it intently, warm and happy and safe.

When I visited the house after she had died, I was aware very much of her absence. And if I was aware, how much worse it must be for you and Bern and Del and Lyn. She had such a strong presence and there's such a big gap now. But mourning the end of a life only happens when the life was worth celebrating. Which Stevie's was. I'm grateful I knew her.

Days after Stevie died I met Del on the path. How are you? I asked. You must be so tired. I'm all right. But I miss Stevie. She dissolved into tears. We hugged each other. I know. So do I.

Stevie, it was after you had died and Bern was still struggling with her cancer, I was sitting with Patrick on the back deck of the ferry. I think it was the end of the day. There is a moment when the ferry engines stop rattling and the ferry starts to glide in towards the pier. It is a moment of great peace. Patrick turned to me, his eyes wide with thought. He is aware that I am tentative on the subject of God but Lyn has certainly indoctrinated him with the orthodox version.

"Do you believe in God?" he has asked on other occasions and I have suggested that it is possible to believe or not to believe, to leave him room to formulate his own catechism, and in any case I don't want to go into the pure nullity that I assume lies at the other side of the gateway of death.

But now, death is a subject that has great meaning for us. Stevie, you have died and Mummy is dying, though we have censored that thought. Patrick needs to comprehend something of this disaster that is happening around him.

"Dad, can I ask you a question?"

"Sure."

"Is it true that, when you're dead, you go up to Heaven and become an angel?"

The questions kids ask. And not being a Christian, I have no belief in Heaven or angels. But what do you tell a child of four coming on five? He needed a picture to explain things. This was as good a picture as any.

"Yes," I said slowly, "I think that's... yes, I'm sure that's the way it is."

Patrick was looking at me intensely. His eyes stared straight into mine.

"How do you know?" he asked.

Oh yes, he'd caught me. I had to laugh and hug him. But he still looked puzzled. It was a real question.

It was the first day of the fog, the Tuesday before the Easter weekend. It happened like this most years. The cool dry winds that were capable of bringing the January and February temperatures down to within a few degrees of frost, winds that I imagined coming all the way down from Siberia, Mongolia, started towards the end of March and early April to be pushed back by wet, warm southerly winds coming in from the Pacific Ocean. The fog wrapped the islands in a virginal embrace of white – a thick, impenetrable, pristine white. The white always made me think of snow and that fresh, mood-enhancing moment on waking to a landscape coated in white. But although my mood should have been light, I was restless with a seething, bitter anger, the frustrated fury of the impotently wretched. I wanted to get home. I'd had to go to work that day but I worked with the heavy feeling I should have been at home – though reason told me there was nothing I could do there. That bloody woman, Clare! That goddamn hospice!

But the fog wrapped me and embraced me and gave me some solace as the ferry churned its way home. My mind was a fog too. Visibility zero. Every day a new catastrophe, a new submerged rock ripped its way into the belly. I was floundering, had been floundering for several months now, maybe longer. What did I know? I was too busy keeping myself afloat to look around me and chart a sensible course.

It had started mid-January. I'd got a call from your mother. She was at the hospital. She wanted me there quick. Why wasn't I there anyway? Why wasn't someone there? My mind is blank. She'd talked to the doctor. It was a regular check-up. The previous one had been fine. Clear. No sign of any of the chemical markers they were checking for. But she was no better in herself. The pain was bad. Added to all the other pains, the pain she had had all year and the pain of the radiation, the chemotherapy – the oedema that made her legs swell up and become painful to the touch – was the new added pain of the stent. The fucking stent. The constant new vocabulary that means pain, that means you weren't fully informed, that means you didn't ask the right questions. A side-effect of the radiation is the likelihood that tubes will be destroyed, like the ureter that carries the urine from the kidneys to the bladder, like the urethra that carries the urine from the bladder out. And if these collapse, then the urine backs up and eventually the kidneys will pack up – and when two kidneys go... and that was Bern's latest problem. And suddenly all the women Bern was talking to in the ward had problems of collapsing urethras that had never been mentioned as potential side-effects before. Why hadn't we met them before? And of course the impossibility of the radiation not hitting anything but the target in the pelvic area with all the complex organic bits and pieces to do with sex and excretion now became glaringly fucking bloody obvious! And that leads us back to the stent. Stenting is the putting of a straw-like device – the stent itself – up the urethra. Bern had been stented. It had been painful. And it wasn't working. She had a catheter so that the urine was collected in a bag. It was all going very slowly and horribly out of control. It was all going very, very wrong. And now this call.

"Come. The doctor says I'm dying."

I found Bern sitting on a bench outside the ward that was her second home.

"He says the cancer's come back. There's nothing they can do. I can't remember everything he said. You talk to him."

But the doctor had gone off somewhere.

"Tell me exactly what he said."

Bern told me again. "He said I'm dying. He said there's nothing more he can do."

She sat shrivelled up like an old woman of seventy or eighty. She was shrinking. She had become so fragile. Every movement aching. And now this. It was clear she was unprepared for it. Why wasn't I there? Why?

"OK. We've come to the end here." Sound positive and in control, I told myself. "Let's do things my way." I wanted to take her straight away to a naturopathic clinic. But Bern refused to move until I too had seen the doctor. She curled up on the bench. The nurses on the ward told me he was in an operation. He would be back at three o'clock. So I sat there – and Bern lay there hugging herself in her own agony – for three hours. She couldn't even bear the pressure of my hand resting on her shoulder, her back, anywhere.

Then the doctor came and we talked. He drew a five inch long sausage wrapped around the left ureter.

"I'm afraid it has come back. We've already radiated this area. Her body couldn't take any more. We could try some more chemotherapy but it would be worse than before and almost certainly it will be no use."

Numb.

There were questions, a great many questions, but the day was getting on and there were things to do. And it was anyway simple enough, she was dying and there was nothing they could do. What was the point any more? We'd waited three or four hours for what? For this... confirmation. But Bern had needed me to hear it.

"How long?"

"Perhaps three months."

"I'm going to prescribe morphine for the pain. Just take as much as you need. Whatever you need to kill the pain. Don't worry, you won't become addicted."

Then, only then, did Bern agree to come with me.

"You really are a fighter, aren't you?" she murmured.

"To the end," I said with all the bravado I could muster but the truth was I felt helpless. All I knew was that we had to keep doing something. But I think Bern gave up that day and she wanted me to give up. She wanted me to hear that she was going to die so that at last I would give up pushing her to take the vitamins and herbs and all the rest of it. But I only know how to persevere, to keep moving forwards, no matter how blindly.

And so we went to the naturopath's clinic. He wanted a urine test and a saliva test done. Bern could produce neither. She sat trying to spit something, anything, into the small plastic container the receptionist had given her. No spit. I had brought her here but I was sick and helpless in the face of this. It took half an hour to produce barely enough to coat the bottom of the container.

So for a few weeks Bern went to the clinic for treatments but then she could no longer make the effort. She stopped going. A friend suggested acupuncture and again she went twice. But it was too late, much too late. The effort of achingly slow, agonising movement was too much for her. To walk ten, fifteen feet took minutes of excruciating effort.

I don't think I was much help after that. I think I pretended we were still fighting. I pretended that we were still on track and that one day it would suddenly be better. Time slowed to the day itself. The future? When was that? What could it offer us? We didn't talk about it. This, so soon after you Stevie! We could not contemplate it. Bern's comfort became the paramount objective. Can I help? I would ask. What do you want to do? What can I get you? Anything to help. Anything to avoid other questions.

Once or twice I got angry with her for not forcing down herbs, vitamins, enzymes and all the other things we were told to do. We were told to drink carrot juice until Bern turned orange. But

Bern couldn't. They made her uncomfortable. She complained she couldn't digest them. And, eventually, I stopped arguing. It wasn't helping.

I have no idea what Bern's thoughts were at this time. I have no memory of what my own thoughts were. I sense in myself a waiting, an absence of thought echoing against itself, reverberating with nothingness, a vacuum of numbed feeling, a resonating pulse of fear and horror just below the threshold of awareness. And sometimes, at night, from the depths of my unhappiness, forbidden thoughts came to me. Maybe it's best if she dies, a voice said and I did not repudiate it. Forgive me. Forgive me.

The pain, of course, was the first priority. I contacted the hospice, which had only recently been established. They had a pain management team. And so Clare, our assigned home care nurse, started to visit us.

Bern felt comforted to have someone take charge. Yes. It is clear we had started to drift. Only what Bern wanted existed. There was no other will, no other force. And Bern stopped taking care of herself and I was blind to it – and if I saw anything at all, consciousness of it must have quickly dissolved in the acid of the silence that lay between us. It became too difficult to confront the immediate facts. And this wouldn't have been so bad, perhaps, if it had simply been pointed out. We would have said: "Oh yes. Of course!"

But it wasn't pointed out.

One day Clare suggested to Bern that she should go into the hospice. She said that she would be more comfortable there. She would be taken care of. There would be blood tests. "What blood tests?" I asked when I was informed of what had now become a firm decision.

"I don't know. Clare said they could do blood tests to see why I'm feeling the way I am."

I was angry that it had all been decided without me being consulted but Bern was firmly set on it. It was definite. The ambulance had been arranged. I had stopped protesting weeks before. Now was not the time to start up again. We arranged for Patrick to go and stay with a friend.

We arrived at the hospice on Friday afternoon and I asked to see the doctor. I wanted some clarifications. I was introduced to the doctor on duty and I immediately set about asking her about the blood tests.

"What blood tests?" she asked.

"I don't know. That's why we're here. My wife is here under the impression that she is here to have blood tests."

"Well, I think she's here to be more comfortable."

"She was comfortable at home."

"You realise that she's dying."

"When? How long?"

"We can't say. Maybe soon."

"What about the blood tests?"

"We can do some tests. They can tell us what is happening. But there's nothing we can do really beyond that."

Then the frustrations started. There weren't enough staff to give Bern the bath she had been promised. Our helpers, Lyn and Del, were taking it in turns to be with her. But they were told they couldn't make tea or get hot water. They offered to give Bern the bath but were told that was against the rules. It was for the nurses to give the baths but there weren't enough nurses. If they wanted anything they had to ask a nurse – and the nurses always looked very busy and it seemed an imposition to keep asking them for all the little things. And it was the weekend so there was no one to give Bern's legs a massage – legs swollen agonizingly with oedema, the build-up of lymph that had to be eased, could only be eased, by massage. Clare came up to see Bern but Bern was now out of her hands as far as responsibility was concerned as she was an out-patient nurse. Bern was now in the hands of the in-patient team. So there was nothing Clare could do to help. It was a classic fuck-up – (I'm sorry Stevie, but there are times when only that word will do) – a decision that may or may not have been sensible had been made in the wrong way and was implemented at the wrong time and no one felt able to reverse the flow of the inevitable. Only I could have done it and I didn't have the designated authority: Bern's blessing to act on her behalf. Bern wanted to stay, so she stayed.

Bern was in a three-person room and one of the other patients was dying – imminently. The family were spending a lot of time around her.

It's one of the aspects of hospitalisation – and hospicisation is no different – that you hand over responsibility for every decision. You accept that there's a system and you fit into it. You become utterly passive. You sink into the passivity. You don't want to be a bother.

The next two days passed but Bern, who had been the dominant, active force was sinking into this passivity and was horrified at my clumsy attempts to arrange things as I thought she might like.

"Don't bother the nurses," she scolded me.

I was woken early on Monday morning. It was Bern's sister, Martha, on the phone.

"Come to the hospital quickly. It's Bern. Something happened last night. I can't explain it."

"What? Is she dead?"

"No. I can't explain. Come quickly."

When I got to the hospital two hours later I was shocked at what I saw. How can I describe it? Bern was a scream that was being screamed inwards into the darkest hollows of the mind, a scream that was prevented from screaming out its agony to the world.

Something had profoundly traumatised her. The muscles in her face were so taut she could barely speak. When she spoke she was barely audible. What she said was totally paranoid. All we could learn from her was that a nurse had tried to kill her in the night. Her face was a mask of grotesque expressions. Her mind was slithering along hallucinatory grooves. From time to time she lay back against her pillow and closed her eyes but the eyes seemed to roll and flicker – rapid eye movements as in a dream state. She said "It's like being in a movie." So, somehow she was aware of us, and that we meant home and safety and comfort.

It took hours to get everything organised to get out.

"What happened?" I asked the nurses. There were no doctors around.

The nurses seemed to be giving us a wide berth. I went to the nurses' desk. There were three nurses busily writing reports.

"My wife. What's happened? I need to talk to someone."

"You can see we're busy."

There are times when the only valid response to events is a scream that obliterates all rationality, a scream of pure infantilism. I should have screamed. But I didn't. I didn't feel I had permission. It was for Bern to scream – but her scream had become petrified in the landscape of her face. So I continued to dither between impotent futility and anger. The decision was quickly made that we were going. An ambulance had to be arranged. That's what we had to wait for. And no one talked to us. The staff avoided us.

And what had happened? It gradually emerged that the woman had started to die very loudly – with great heavings and pantings – at three o'clock in the morning. Bern had woken up, seen what was happening and then, according to one nurse, she turned her face to the pillow and the death became her own death – and she was not in her own bed surrounded by her own things. She was in enemy territory where the nurses had dispossessed her of her being, of her power to order the world as she wanted. And there was an emotional seizure. One of the doctors later said it was a common state known as terminal confusion.

But he was wrong.

We took Bern home and the further we got from the hospice the more she relaxed. But even as we eased her into her own bed in her own bedroom, she remained taut with the extreme agony of her experience.

That had been Monday. Now it was Tuesday. We woke. I helped her out of bed and we slowly, with creaking, measured steps, made our way out to the sitting room. Bern was looking much better, much more relaxed. My heart went out to her.

"There are some things that are clear to me but there are some things I don't understand."

I didn't understand what she meant by this and I tried to make a joke of it.

"There are a lot of things I don't understand too."

She stopped near the dining table and looked about her and then looked at me with a very sweet apologetic smile.

"Do we live here?" she asked.

And my heart nearly broke.

And now it was Tuesday evening. I was coming back home. It was a ten-minute walk from the ferry pier home. And there was a good feeling with the fog all around, sitting in tree branches and in the valleys. I wondered how I would find Bern.

As I entered the flat I could hear her talking to someone. It was Clare. I came up the short flight of stairs from the front door. Bern was sitting at the table with her back to me, leaning against the banisters. I touched her shoulder gently, to let her know I was there.

"I'm very angry with you Clare," I said straight away, glaring at her, but Clare did not respond. There was a momentary pause as she kept her eyes on Bern. Then she spoke, not to me and my anger but to Bern, carrying on the conversation they were having. My anger surged and became a tight knot in my throat. But, at the same time, I sensed that something momentous was happening. It was best not to interrupt. My anger could wait.

"Do you know what's happening?" she asked.

"I'm a bit confused," Bern admitted.

"Do you want to know what's happening to you?"

"What's happening?"

"You're dying. You're going to die very soon."

Bern seemed suddenly to waken to this reality. And I did too.

"This is a shock," Bern said.

Tears were coursing down my face and I squeezed Bern's shoulder and caressed the back of her neck.

"How do you feel about this?" Clare was leaning forward intently. This is what she had come to do. She had come to open the door to Bern's dying. And she did it. My anger crumbled and I was washed with gratitude to her for what she was doing.

"I never expected this." I could feel her surprise.

"How do you feel?" Clare persisted.

"I don't know."

"Is there anything you need to do?"

"How long?"

"I can't say. But you don't have very long. A few days."

"I never expected this. It's a shock."

I too felt the shock at this sudden immediacy.

"There are practical things. Like money and so on. You need to think carefully about what you need to do." Clare knew her job was to get this truth through to us.

And Easter weekend was coming, so it was just two days to do everything in.

Yes, there were bank things to do. My signature had to be added to some accounts she had that I hadn't known about. And there was her family in Canada.

"Oh Bern. I want to hold you in my arms all night and just hug you tight."

"No," she said. "Just as we always do." Touching lightly. Holding hands lightly. In this way she reminded me of her pain.

I called Martha and she called Bern's brothers and sisters in Canada. Later she called back to say that Charles and Brian had arranged to fly over and would be arriving on the Saturday morning. We told Bern. Martha and Vivian and Sherman arrived the next day.

On Wednesday, Bern said she wanted to die soon. The pain was so great. And I thought about this meaningless pain. It served no purpose. Nothing could be learnt from it. It could not serve to change a person's fate. It was a pain that took all Bern's energy just to cope with it. I know in her mind she had resolved to stay alive to say goodbye to her brothers. But that done, then she would allow herself to die. And in the meanwhile there was this pain.

It was Wednesday night that we gave her more morphine. The air was dank, humid. We lay on the bed, sticky, touching, barely touching, while Martha and Vivian took it in turns to mop faces with cooling cloths. They were there to serve us and I was there to touch Bern lightly so that she would know I was there. We felt very close to each other though we hardly spoke a word. The immensity of what might be said was so great and yet, what after all was there to say that wasn't being said by look and touch.

It was three or four in the morning. Suddenly Bern sat up in bed and started laughing. She wanted to phone the Queen of Mexico. She wanted to know where I was hiding the castles. She knew I had them. She demanded I show her them. Martha laughed.

"Where did that dream come from?"

This was the morphine talking.

Patrick had been staying with some friends so we asked them to bring him back. Five years old and he had lost you, his sister, already. Now his mother. It wasn't fair. I took him for a walk and told him his mother was dying. He didn't react much and seemed relieved when I arranged for him to go off and play with a friend. Friends came by to say goodbye. And Bern seemed almost to be shrinking day by day, but she was so pleased to be able to say goodbye to her old friends.

Somehow there was a need for music but Bern had never shown any interest in music before. I put on a CD of Christmas songs by the Chieftains and turned the sound down low so that it was barely audible. After a while, I noticed that Bern was smiling and swivelling a finger in the air.

"You're enjoying it?" I said in surprise.

"Too late," she said. "I never heard it before."

And so for the next few days we played it over and over again, constantly. It nearly drove us mad but it was the soundtrack of her last days and I think she got some pleasure from it.

Those few days seemed almost happy with a kind of heightened humour. With her friends she had a light gaiety along with her natural graciousness. I remember saying once: "If you're not careful you might actually get well again." And we all thought this was hilarious.

I remember noting that Bern's eyes had changed. The intense flickering that had started in the hospice gradually ceased, to be replaced by a wide-eyed staring. They had become black impenetrable islands in translucent grey liquid pools. And her face was mobile with disquieting distastes. But she never spoke of them and I preferred not to focus attention on anything unpleasant. Better to sit in a silence of empathy.

I was worried she would die in the night but we had to sleep. I remember nights of fitful dreaming then waking then waking again and knowing I had been dreaming, a sleep as light and restless as butterfly wings.

On the Friday, she spoke to me clearly for the first time showing that she understood.

"Ju-ju," her name for me, little pig, "You must marry again and give Patrick a mother. He needs a mother."

Yes. The vacuum that is about to engulf us. The rock of certainty that Bern was, about to leave me stranded on the shores of life. How was it going to be? Replaced? Impossible to imagine. Impossible to consider. Perhaps I welcomed the coming emptiness. I shook my head.

"No, ju-ju, you must."

But it was an idea that could not be thought of. Not now.

And all week we felt wrapped as if packaged in cotton wool by the thick fog outside. It hemmed us in. Our flat was a stage where momentous events were taking place. There was no distance. There was no real world out there. Everything was here in this room. All consciousness. It was a play. Everything was pre-ordained. A ritual. We were, simply, the performers, acting out the parts – of which nothing could be changed – performing ourselves for ourselves.

Each day Bern woke and her first words were: "I can't stand this any more." But we were all wrapped in the cloak of the inevitability of this Greek tragedy. It would last as long as it had to and then the end would come. The script was clear. She would die soon after Charles and Brian arrived. We all expected this.

Françoise had arranged to meet them at the airport and drop them off at the ferry pier. At 10:45 they arrived at the door. Bern was already reclining in a rattan lounging chair that was the only place she felt comfortable. At around midday, on cue, following the hidden script, she suddenly started to feel panicky.

"Quick everyone! Hold my hand."

We all knelt beside her and held her hands and lay our hands on her arms and shoulders. All of us: Two sisters, two brothers, two brothers-in-law and a husband clutched her hands and waited. She closed her eyes. We waited... and waited... and waited. Twenty, twenty-five minutes passed. Nothing happened.

"She's not dying yet," Martha said.

We slowly let out a communal breath, a release, and disentangled ourselves. Even Bern was surprised. It had seemed the perfect moment. Everything would have been completed. But, now that the moment had passed, it was time for lunch. Suddenly we all felt cast adrift. Nothing was certain any more, nothing that is, except the fact that Bern was not going to die today. I remember going out for a walk, to get something. There must have been a light smile on my face, perhaps a certain jaunty humour in my expression. I met a friend on the path.

"How's it going?" he asked. A neutral uncommitted question.

"Great!" I said, and I could almost see his head jerk back. "Bern's not going to die today," I told him. "She's going to die tomorrow." And I walked on gaily, shaking my head at myself at how weird that had sounded and yet that was how I felt. Maybe, she'll die during the night, I thought. I lay on my side and watched her, making sure I would be there for her when it happened. Her eyes stared straight ahead unblinking for hours – but, Sunday morning, when I said she hadn't slept at all, Martha laughed and said of course she had slept. So obviously I had slept as well.

Dawn came that Sunday morning and suddenly Bern had a great burst of energy. She started to order everyone around.

"Get me up! I said get me up! Are you stupid?" We got her up and laid her on the couch. What now? Suddenly it seemed possible that she might just have decided that she was going to get well again. She was capable of anything. She lay there resting all morning. Patrick went to play with a friend. What could he be making of all this? Then sometime just before half past twelve she suddenly had a great need for her leg to be massaged.

"Hurry, hurry!" she called out and at the same moment she clutched her chest. A terrible pain seemed to be travelling up through her. We didn't know whether it was for her leg to be massaged or for death to take her that she was calling out. And she started to pant with heavy loud heaving gasps. The phone rang. It was Bern's friend Suzanne who was looking after Patrick. I told her not to bring Patrick. I felt that the sight of Bern dying would be too disturbing for him. But ten minutes later, prompted perhaps by some instinct, she called back and I told her Bern was going and to bring Patrick up as Bern would want to say goodbye to him. And so Patrick came up and there seemed to be a pause in events as we told him to hug his mother and to say goodbye to her. He hugged her.

"Goodbye Mummy," he said and kissed her cheek.

"Are you OK?" I asked as I led him to the door. He seemed to nod but I saw he couldn't take it in. He struggled to put his shoes on. So I said hug her again and he did. What could he understand of it all? Suzanne led him away. But Bern's breathing had quieted dramatically, the distress had gone. All of us held her hands. This time there was no doubt about it. This time it was for real.

"Say something! Talk to her," Lyn sobbed to us and we all did. And then her breathing became so quiet it was inaudible and then, soon after, she left us.

"Go in peace, Bern. Go in peace."

It was just after ten past one on Easter Sunday.

Death takes a lot of getting used to and we felt in no hurry. It was over. It – the unspeakable 'it' – had finally happened. Martha and Vivian set about cleaning her and dressing her in a new dress, to ready her for her next journey. And then we had lunch.

It was a slow afternoon. We lay Bern on the settee and all of us spent time with her. She was at peace. She was out of her pain at last. And I looked out the window and I saw the fog begin to clear and within an hour it had gone.

It may be that there is a touch of farce in all death. At four thirty we finally got round to calling the emergency services. The tiny village ambulance came with the rescue team. They burst in the door – keystone cops-like – and rushed over to her with an oxygen mask to attempt resuscitation. We assured them it wasn't necessary. They assured us it was their job, they had to do it. We told them they'd done it. By this time Bern was quite rigid. I was surprised at this. Stevie, you remained soft for such a long time. Then they took Bern away and I had to make a report to the police.

"And who else was with you and your wife when she died?" the plain-clothes detective asked.

"Her two sisters, two of her brothers, two brothers-in-law, my maid."

He nodded: foul play was not suspected, he assured me.

Sherman, who throughout the dying had been a quiet peripheral presence, now took charge to lay down the law of traditional observances. Bern's spirit would return to the house one evening. He guessed it would be the third. On that day, I was to spread things that she particularly liked around the sitting room – and to set aside some food. So that she would be undisturbed, we had to close our doors. We did as instructed but I queried why I wasn't to open the door. Sherman was insistent that this would be very bad. I didn't hear anything that night.

Later, Sherman went to a fortune teller and was told that Bern had already been reborn as a Goddess and that she would return on the Saturday after the funeral. So once again I laid everything out but again I had no sense of her coming back. However, three weeks later, suddenly, at four in the morning, I was woken by the television turning itself on and humming with the blue screen lit up. I sat up straight.

"Hello, is that you Bern?" I spoke out loud to the surrounding dark, feeling half silly and yet that it might be possible.

"We love you. Patrick's all right. Are you all right?"

There was no answer and after a minute or two I turned the television off. That had never happened before.

Almost a year later, the first night in the bed with another woman – the attempt, too soon, to enter a new relationship – feeling multiply strange: at the newness of the contact of flesh again, a palpable sense of breaking boundaries, yes, also, the sense of betrayal. Once again, at three in the morning, the sudden humming of the blue screen as the television switched itself on.

"Bern? Is that you?" I spoke aloud to the blackness.

My companion was wide awake, wide-eyed and thoroughly spooked.

"Bern, this is Katie. She's my new friend."

But there was no response. There was only the middle of the night silence and the humming blue screen. It hasn't happened since. Maybe she felt it was time for her to move on too.

Ghosts make strange appearances. Three years later, I pulled an old camera out of a drawer where it had languished. I noticed that there was still some film in it so I had it developed. Much of the film had spoiled but one frame remained crisply clear. Stevie, it was Patrick's birthday party, seven weeks after you died. There was your mother supervising the games, as she loved to do. She had drawn a large donkey and was organising the kids for Put the Tail on the Donkey. Six weeks earlier, at your funeral, Stevie, Bern had looked stylish and strong in an air-force blue beret. Now, here in this photo, I saw how thin and weak she had become in such a short time. I saw what everyone around us must have seen except me, something inevitable, her slow dying.

Louise told me later something of what she remembered of these last days of Bern's.

I remember one night, when I had some banking stuff for you – taking the papers to your home. It can't have been many days before Bern died. I walked into a house full of people, none of whom I recognised – not even the one who greeted me. It was Bern. Ethereal and 'other' and beautiful. (That night, I finally found you on the roof, talking to the social worker. The atmosphere was strangely rather jolly.)

I think it's true to say that you probably make your own death to some extent. Bern was translucently serene. She waited for her brothers – she lay, radiant, in the middle of the living room and beamed her goodbyes to everyone. I left crying but now I remember her joy. Maybe it was realising how beloved she was.

The funeral too was not without farce. The gang of labourers that had been hired to carry the coffin set out at a great pace and would not be restrained. It was a mile walk to the crematorium. A line of some hundred or so mourners, we soon found ourselves strung out in a long line, Patrick and I in the lead, sweating, up a hill and then down to the crematorium building set among the graves of the cemetery, overlooking the islands to the south.

For those of us who have no firm religious structures to clasp at times like this, a funeral poses problems. A Christian service would have done nothing for me. Instead, several friends spoke of their feelings for Bern, spoke of their memories, spoke of her wide, endearing smile. I said a few words about how this handmade funeral was our humble attempt to do something appropriate to register the mystery of death. We sang Bern's favourite song, because it was your favourite song, Stevie. *Twinkle twinkle little star, how I wonder what you are...*

Afterwards, we turned to Chinese folk practices and lit joss sticks and burnt offerings: a miniature house, a paper television, a boat, two servants and a paper car (Bern had just passed her driving test when she first heard she had cancer). She would need a car to drive around Heaven. A neighbour apologised for his wife's absence but said it was against her deepest religious beliefs. My mouth fell open in surprise. I went over to a group of friends and invited them to burn offerings, if it wasn't against their deepest beliefs. Gavin replied with the wonderful words: "Jonathan, it is not against my deepest religious beliefs, but even if it were, I would still do it."

"Were you there when Mummy disappeared?" Patrick asked me when we told him she had gone. I think he had some vision of her rising lightly towards the sun and the light. I explained that she had been taken to the hospital.

"Do you believe in God, Daddy?" Patrick asked me some days or weeks later. I hummed and hawed and said this was an area that many people had different ideas about.

"There must be a God," he said.

"Why?"

"Because he took Mummy to live with him."

I agreed that this was good thinking. A week later Patrick declared that there wasn't a God, but he didn't elaborate. Then he asked for clarification.

"When Mummy goes to Heaven does she stay with God or does she become God?"

"That's an interesting question."

On another day Patrick asked: "Does everybody die?"

"Yes, they do."

"Except me!" he said.

"Oh yes?"

"Young people don't die."

"That's true," I said and wished it were.

Death and dying are a strange and exhausting business. But living has to go on. The day after the funeral, Patrick and I spent the day on a boat. I was feeling fragile from too much to drink and the sadness of the empty bed and the hollow pillow I hugged all night, exhausted above all with having too little time to feel the grief that I felt I should be feeling. But there were, and had been and continued to be, too many contrary tides of energy. It had been a hard year. There was more than a smattering of relief that it was all over. Perhaps that shouldn't be said but truth and reality are rarely simple or direct or uncluttered. We always feel the pangs of hunger or the urge to pee at the wrong moment. There is no point denying that or pretending to feelings that aren't felt. Life and consciousness are blowing through us and it is best if we don't attach ourselves too hard to the here and now but simply acknowledge the flow as it is flowing.

Patrick and I returned to the house after dark. We had forgotten to leave a light on. We rounded the corner and it hit us both at the same moment: the dark lonely emptiness of the flat. Just nine months earlier it had housed a community of four adults and two children. Now only the two of us were left.

"It's so empty," Patrick said, putting words to the fact.

"Never mind, come on," I said, false jollying him along, putting a note of decisive certainty into my voice. I unlocked the front door and quickly switched on all the lights. It felt better straight away. It was a sticky night and we were hot and sweaty from the day on the water. I turned on the air-conditioner. There was an immediate clunk and the whole house was plunged back into darkness. A bloody fuse! It was as if some field of subtle energy had unwrapped itself and left the house and the electrical system was responding to this fact. If Bern had been there it wouldn't have happened. Patrick screamed.

"Why did you do that? Why did you do it?"

"Never mind. We'll go to Louise's house and you can sleep there." I managed, I hope, to sound calm and assured. And we left the house and it seemed like the perfectly apt, perfectly awful end to a terrible time.

One is never adequate to the grief. The bitter gift of the loss of a life does not weigh so heavily as it should for as long as it should. Forever. Absolutely. Today and tomorrow and always. We choose life and recovery. We close the door and forget. We turn our backs. We betray the memory. From time to time perhaps a cock crows but we have our tricks of thought and subtle justifications... and of course we are sorry. So very sorry. But we are made of stuff that rises, that lifts. And I am so very sorry.

And life hurtles us forward to the next moment of pain, the next tragicomic scenario. Because we are human. The next moment of pure idiocy that undermines our conceits. We. Us. Our.

I am, Stevie, as you know, talking of myself. I seek frail comfort in extending my fate to the whole human world.

And what, in the end, Stevie, can I say? I can show you no product. The pain, as with the love, is its own justification. The feeling of it the only objective. There is no philosophy at the end, no message. If there is an increase in wisdom it is not a wisdom that can be spoken of. It is the wisdom of the heart – a wisdom that fate continues to mock – a heaviness in the soul that makes us walk out of step with the world. There are, too, occasional glimpses of distant happinesses, long ago cauterized. I remember Louise's letter. Noble? Surely it was the spacey dissociation of the punch-drunk boxer too dumb and confused to fall down.

Sometimes I go up to my flat roof and gaze down at the small rocky inlet below the flat. Here there is a small stretch of sand hedged around by rock. In the middle of the coarse sand is a small altar shaped plug of rock. This is nature's altar that I have taken over as my own memorial for you, Stevie, and for Bern. One day I hope it will be there for me too. It was here we laid your photo, and Bern's photo. It was here we laid the flowers and the pitiful, small cotton bags that contained your ashes. It was here that I tried vainly to give proper weight to the moment, to feel properly the heavy weight of the grief. But I was blank and empty. I only knew that I wanted to perform the ritual. I took the ashes and dissolved them slowly in the sea. The water was cool and refreshing as it came up to my knees. I pulled out a handful of the ashes – powdery, gritty – and stirred it into the sea. Then others around me started casting flowers into the sea. The water lapped at shallow rocks. More ashes. The incoming and outgoing of the sea soon spread the flowers like a carpet over a stretch of water going out, into the bay. I imagined the particles of ash dissolved in the sea going out with them – going out to the ocean – and mixing with the grains of sand under my feet – dissolving into the entire universe, joining once again with the earth. You. And two people say they saw a large fish out in the bay leap out of the water. I have watched the waters of this bay for many hours and I have never seen a fish. Maybe it came to collect your spirit and take you to the submarine palaces of the blessed. Maybe it was just a fish that leaped out of the sea startled by the subtle change in the world's energy as you dissolved into it. Maybe it was just a fish randomly sporting. Just a moment of coincidental connection. Just you. Just a fish. Just me. Just all of us, a whole community, gathered in the rocky inlet to pay homage to your life, your death; your being among us for a while and then going, leaving us with subtle lessons. For once we know something, it is impossible to imagine not knowing it. And Stevie, you made us know something huge.

I have no need of any other afterworld. To have my ashes dissolved in the sea is an after death fate that I welcome for myself. To become one with the flux of the tides and the rhythm of planets. One day, when my own ashes have joined the same sea, my own atoms will jostle with Bern's and yours, Stevie, and we will join together in one body and this body will travel along new paths of love and pain.

If only we could know it. If only we could be greater than we are. But we're not. And the affairs of the world reclaim us, and we sink once again into the world of habit and everyday intrigue.

As I write, four years later, looking back on this moment, this life that we shared together, Patrick and I live our quiet life alone with each other. I think we prefer it this way. Who else could fit into the harmony of understanding we have? But as I say these words, I sense they are mere bravado. The fact is we are incomplete. Together – the four of us – we were whole, now we are fragmented and more than a little lost. But the pain of trying to put together another wholeness – a wholeness that excludes you, the two of you – is too much. It's hard to imagine it. I tried once. It was a mistake. Perhaps a necessary mistake. Even bad mistakes can have good fruit. Shall I try again? Not for a while yet at least. Looking back at this time, I shake my head at the bewilderment of emotions. First there had been that extraordinary sense of release, like a helium balloon suddenly untethered, floating upwards, uncertain as to direction but light and airy. Oh yes. The sense of release. And then the need to just plug on, continue with the everyday, hold tight to work and habits and schedules that kept life solid and anchored. What a strange combination, this floating and this holding on. And then slowly becoming wrapped in that strange feeling that I existed in a vacuum, surrounded by unfeeling space. It seemed to me that I could think clearly, if simply; in here, in this brain where I was, I had no feelings, no emotions, just a simple, clear, perhaps slightly slow, mind. And outside, out there, where the world was, there was a kind of buzzing chaos. But I felt completely separate from it and found I had no feeling that I needed to relate to it. No, that's too simple. I was there but I was also not there. I was simultaneously engaged but disconnected. I didn't respond quickly. Too often my mind and emotions were a complete blank to me. This space I occupied, on reflection, was a simple, and not in any way terrifying, emptiness. I felt brain damaged. I knew that the way I was responding was not the way one should respond but I had little idea of what kind of response I should be giving – and was not always aware that a response was expected. I am only just now emerging. And still there is the sense of damage, possibly permanent. Not metaphoric damage. Real damage. Dead brain cells. Synapses that have shrivelled and become desiccated.

But it may be that I am healing. In the past few weeks I have had the following dreams. It is to do with writing this book. Lots of dreams – every night it seems – which is strange considering I never remembered my dreams before.

Stevie, I found myself lying beside you and I thought "This is wonderful. It seems so long since I had done this. Too long." And then you curled up and pulled the covers over your shoulder and said "I'm sleepy" and I marvelled at the movements and the words. You could speak! How was it that I didn't know that? Now, I said to myself, now I can speak to you and you'll understand me. And for a long time I lay with the golden feeling that you were still with us. And then, slowly, reluctantly, I came to understand it was just a dream and I was heavy with sadness.

And another early morning, I woke with a strong sense of guilt. I had been neglectful. I hadn't seen Bern for such a long time. She was at her sister, Martha's. I hadn't phoned her for so long. We hadn't talked. She must be angry with me. I couldn't blame her. I had to phone her straight away. Oh God, yes. And then it came to me why we hadn't talked for so long. And it was two o'clock in the morning.

I had another dream. I was in a place. I was restless. So I got on a bus and went to another place. And I met Bern. And Bern had left me for some reason in the past. And I wasn't coping well on my own. And we talked. I got the message that she wanted us to be together again. Yes, it seemed to me that we should be together again. I was happy that we were going to be together again. We had been apart too long. I woke up happy at the decision. Then I understood it was a dream and that Bern was still dead.

And at the end, I am alone in the flat overlooking the rocks where a heavy, regular, creamy swirling sea flows over the rocks and up the small stretch of sand, clutching at the rough quartz and debris of broken shells and pottery that make up the foreshore. Patrick is off somewhere playing with his friends. He is a happy boy and seems to have the knack of ignoring the weight of melancholy that I cannot shift from my shoulders. But we go on from day to day and I pretend to be solid and clear. And somehow we have survived and continue to survive. And I had thought death would be an ending, that mourning would be simple and soon over, that Bern's dying would be a solution to the continuing unhappiness. But that's not how it has been.

And Patrick too has not forgotten. Every evening he asks me seemingly meaningless questions – what's your all time favourite food? What's your favourite film? What's the best cartoon hero? And so on. But in amongst them are questions in disguise. If you could have anything you wanted what would you choose? Oh I don't know. What would I choose? The truth is I have few wants. I have had wanting things beaten out of me. So I turn the question back. "What about you? What would you choose?" I ask him. "I'd like Stevie and Mummy to be with us again."

Ah yes! That! Patrick too remembers and feels sad.

The path of my life goes on ahead into the future, over hills and down into distant invisible valleys. I don't know what adventures there are but even though I am lost I am at ease. I have had the worst. Please God I have had the worst.

Oh Stevie! What a series of stories you led us down; paths through such tangles of hurt; fearful and scary. Such paths as the most frightening of fairy tales tell us of.

A few weeks or months after Bern died, Patrick and I went on holiday. We treated ourselves to a Club Med resort on the east coast of Malaysia. Here there was a path that took you down from the main building to the beach through a half-tamed jungle. It was our second or third day and I took Patrick's hand and I said to him, "Come on. Let's walk down this path through the forest to..." I had no sooner got the word 'forest' out of my mouth when I knew it was the wrong word. Forest. The word breathed fear. He had heard this fairy tale before. It was one of the scary ones like Goldilocks and the Three Bears. Father takes child deep into the forest. This was Hansel and Gretel. Patrick shrieked and pulled. He would not take another step. Poor Patrick. But the power of story is very strong, and who could blame him? I never did get him to go down that path. Who knows what mines we might have stepped on, what witches in icing-coated cottages we might have stumbled upon? Life cannot be trusted not to blow up in our faces. It is, as Patrick well knows, capable of the most unimaginable horror.

So Stevie, now, I think, it is time for me to move on. It's time to say goodbye to you. Take care of your mother as she will be taking care of you. Give her my love too. One day we will all be together again. Goodbye Stevie. Goodbye Bern. I will be with you both soon enough. You will wait for me. There is no hurry. We are and always will be part of the same universe.

And there is one more thing. Something that still needs to be said. Stevie, Bern. Thank you. Thank you for everything.